The Secret to Developing Peak Performers

Get the Best from Your People

NATIONAL PRESS PUBLICATIONS

A Division of Rockhurst University Continuing Education Center, Inc.
6901 West 63rd Street • P.O. Box 2949 • Shawnee Mission, Kansas 66201-1349
1-800-258-7248 • 1-913-432-7757

The Secret to Developing Peak Performers —
Get the Best from Your People

Published by National Press Publications, Inc.
Copyright 2000 National Press Publications, Inc.
A Division of Rockhurst University Continuing Education Center, Inc.

Printed in the United States of America

 5 6 7 8 9 10

ISBN 1-55852-274-3

Table of Contents

INTRODUCTION

Every organization today seeks stellar performance from its employees. Only through outstanding productivity and innovation can a company thrive and even survive in our ever-changing, fast-paced world.

What differentiates peak performers from the average worker? Management consultants have spent decades trying to figure that out.

- Are peak performers smarter?

- Are they more self-confident?

- Do they have better interpersonal skills?

- Do they have better leadership skills?

- Do they have more drive?

- Do they just have the right job or the right boss?

The answer to each of these questions is NO! It's not the talents and skills they possess that make them different ... it's what they do with them that makes the difference.

Everyone knows what it takes to achieve peak performance — initiative, networking, self-management and teamwork. But, those who excel in the corporate environment have a fundamentally different understanding of what these words mean. Peak performers define them like this:

Initiative:

Doing something above and beyond their job.

Helping others.

Taking risks.

Seeing an activity through to completion.

Networking:

Cultivating relationships with people who have knowledge and information they need.

Recognizing that they have expertise others need.

Acknowledging that networking is a bartering process.

Self-management:

Managing time efficiently.

Selecting high-profile projects in the company's critical path.

Maintaining a healthy perspective.

Perpetually expanding their knowledge base.

Teamwork:

Focusing on group rather than individual success.

Bringing organizational savvy to the work process.

Leading by example.

Communicating openly across the board.

Internalizing and maintaining that degree of intense commitment to excellence is a tall order for employees, especially during an era when well over 50 percent of the work force is experiencing burnout. Management's responsibility is to assist by providing support and encouragement … and motivation.

1 MOTIVATION AS A LEADERSHIP TOOL

As an overworked manager, you may feel that motivating your employees is not your problem. Ensuring your department's productivity and meeting bottom-line requirements are your job responsibilities, not all this nonsense about recognition and team building. Staying motivated is up to each of your employees. After all, they possess some of the greatest motivators around: a regular paycheck, job security and company benefits.

Then take it from a pro, "the prince of positive thinking" Tommy Lasorda. As manager of the world champion Los Angeles Dodgers, he realized motivation didn't automatically come with a high-dollar salary or an impressive position. "People say, 'you mean to tell me you've got a guy making $1.5 million a year and you've got to motivate him?' I say absolutely. Everybody needs to be motivated. Everybody from the President of the United States on down."

In this chapter, we'll look at the difference between "job satisfiers" and what genuinely motivates employees to do their best.

Job Satisfiers vs. Motivators

A Rutgers University study revealed a dynamic value shift in the work force that has created a motivation gap — the difference between what managers think their employees want and what employees actually want.

Employees were given a list of 10 job factors and asked to rank them in importance from one to 10. Managers and supervisors were given the same list and asked to rank them the way they thought their employees would. The results were very illuminating. The managers and supervisors were often completely wrong about what really mattered most to their employees.

In the past, management considered employees' needs to be met by the traditional trio: raises, promotions and job security. Now all that is changing. Eighty percent of today's work force values more "inner-directed" job motivators.

Money and perks are effective in the recruiting stage of attracting top candidates to a company, but they do not work as long-term motivators. Salaries, benefits, promotions, working conditions, and company policies are basically job satisfiers. They keep workers satisfied with their jobs, but they don't inspire them to go the extra mile.

Employees are motivated by having their basic needs met not just for survival, but for social and spiritual growth as well. Today's workers also are interested in work as a means of self-fulfillment. According to the Rutgers University study, employees really want:

1. To be treated with respect.

2. An opportunity for personal growth.

3. Self-expression in work and in life.

4. Allowances made for individual preferences and needs.

5. A positive work environment that values employees as individuals.

6. Information about the company's decisions and policies.

Maslow's Hierarchy of Needs

These needs closely parallel the hierarchy of needs defined by psychologist Abraham Maslow in *Motivation and Personality*. Maslow argued that people are motivated by different levels of needs, and that lower-level needs must be met before higher-level needs. Maslow's hierarchy identified five levels of needs, listed in order below:

1. Basic biological or physical needs. These needs include hunger, thirst and sleep. The workplace isn't where such needs are directly met. However, a paycheck is the symbolic way in which employees assure themselves of food and shelter.

2. Need for safety and security. Employees can find a commitment to safety and security when their work environment incorporates fair play, job tenure, job protection, and insurance.

3. Belonging and social activity. Man is a social creature. It's part of his social development to find satisfaction in belonging to and being accepted by a group. Often, that group consists of one's co-workers. Rather than discouraging subordinates from socializing at work, managers can capitalize on this need by utilizing it to build strong teams.

4. Enjoying esteem and status. The desire for status, recognition, respect, and acknowledgment of accomplishment are strong needs for many employees. Once they have acquired a certain expertise and made a significant contribution, they need to be rewarded. Savvy managers initiate ways to recognize employees' contributions.

5. Self-realization and fulfillment. This last set of needs is the most likely to be overlooked by both employees and managers. People often defer the pursuit of self-fulfillment because they are too busy satisfying social or status needs. Good managers understand their employees and know what it will take to help them achieve personal fulfillment.

Motivating by Fulfilling Needs

In the old days, bosses could use fear and coercion as motivators. The boss yelled and the work got done. There was always the explicitly stated or silently implied threat of the employee's job hanging in the balance.

Today's managers realize that effective motivation is no longer simply a matter of dangling a carrot on a stick before their workers, providing financial rewards and penalizing failure. They achieve the greatest success by:

1. Making sure basic needs are met (pay, benefits, job security).

2. Creating a work climate where employees are given opportunities to fulfill their higher-level needs (social, esteem, self-fulfillment).

What Do Employees Want?

No matter how mundane or repetitious, employees want their jobs to be challenging. They also want to derive personal meaning from their work. They need to know they're using their abilities to do a good job at something that is genuinely important.

Take a look at the people you manage and ask yourself whether their jobs incorporate the following criteria for satisfaction:

1. The job isn't monotonous to workers. They can change the pace by varying their tasks.

2. The job doesn't waste employees' time and effort. Management has planned work in such a way that energy isn't exerted uselessly.

3. Workers feel free to plan their own work and the ways to do it most effectively.

4. Workers feel they have a reasonable degree of authority and autonomy over how their work is done.

5. Workers can correct their own errors and improve their own techniques.

6. Workers don't feel too closely supervised, over-instructed or rigidly controlled by management.

7. Workers see their work as an integral part of the whole company. Each worker is valued as an individual, not as a cog in the machine.

8. Feedback from supervisors isn't embarrassing to workers. If it's praise, it's made public. If it's criticism, it's given in private.

People-Friendly Policies

According to Korn/Ferry International, an executive search firm, the workaholic syndrome that put top performers out in front a decade ago is fading away. More workers today are looking for companies that are family-friendly. This means offering a flexible work schedule so employees can share in important family events, secure decent care for dependents (elderly family members and children), and lead more fulfilled lives outside the workplace. To be effective, today's managers have to understand how to implement these changes. To be competitive, today's companies have to offer employees a range of work options unheard of in the past.

Whether or not your company's policies reflect the concerns of its employees, you as a manager need to be sensitive to your staff's needs in balancing their home and work lives. By demonstrating your acceptance of the fact that the personal lives of your staff don't disappear at the office door, you'll be a more effective manager and better motivator. Here are six ways you can implement new policies and facilitate existing ones.

1. Determine your employees' personal needs. Don't assume you already know their needs. Do a needs assessment. Ask:

   • How many of your employees are parents with child-care needs?

- How many are responsible for elderly parents?

- What could you or the company be doing to help employees with family-life concerns?

2. Look at time in a new way. Consider initiating:

   - Flextime. Consider a new look at scheduling: for instance, allowing employees to arrive as early as 7 a.m. or staying until 6 p.m. Once set, the schedule needs to be regular.

   - Job sharing.

   - Working at home. Allowing employees to work at home often produces the same or better results than rigid work schedules.

3. Make policies that match reality. When working parents need to stay home with sick children, they often use sick time. If the policy is strictly defined to include only the time an employee is sick, it encourages dishonesty. Give employees personal time that they can use to take care of personal business matters or sick relatives.

4. If dependent care isn't offered, initiate flexible benefits. Some small companies give their employees annual allowances that can be applied to child care. A childless employee might apply the allowance toward a health club membership. Or, offer flexible spending accounts whereby employees can spend a portion of their before-tax earnings on dependent care.

5. Get the backing of other managers. If your company resists change, get other departmental managers to support family-related benefits.

6. When employees make special requests, listen. If employees propose a change, such as working at home or job sharing, it may require the approval of unions, CEOs, sales managers, district managers, etc. Give your employees support to prove that an unusual work arrangement can succeed.

Key Points

- Employees must feel they're working for a company that cares about them and their needs. They need to feel they're partners in making the business work.

- Communicating this to your employees is a lot of work, but it comes with a big payoff.

- Employees who feel their company needs them, cares about them, and shares important information with them are your most valuable asset.

- Motivated employees can turn a sliding profit margin around, advertise your company, and keep you and your staff motivated and on track. Your job is to let it happen.

In the following chapters, we'll look at ways to improve motivation — what works and what doesn't — through team building, communication, delegation, recognition, and financial incentives. You can also assess how motivated you are and whether your company is doing all it can to ensure that its employees are happy, well-compensated and free to do the best job possible.

1. How do you and your company show your employees that the company cares about them as individuals, not just for what they can do for the organization?

2. How can you more effectively communicate this to each employee?

3. Jot down your ideas for improving your employees' motivation through:

   • team building.

   • communication.

   • delegation.

   • recognition.

   • financial incentives.

4. Now read the remainder of this handbook to expand upon your ideas.

Reflections

2 ARE YOU A MOTIVATED MANAGER?

You've done everything possible to pump up your staff, from weekly pep talks to one-on-one meetings. Yet nothing seems to work. When you push for higher productivity, they tackle their jobs with all the enthusiasm of a chain gang. When you try the opposite tactic and lessen the pressure, they spend all their time chatting, and indulging in extra-long lunches and personal phone calls.

What's wrong? Why aren't you able to motivate your staff more effectively?

The problem may be you. If you're not a motivated leader, your employees are the first to know. In this chapter, we'll determine how motivated you really are. We'll take a look at:

- What motivation consists of and what the difference is between external and internal motivators.

- How you can improve your self-esteem.

- How your personal mission statement matches your company's.

- The characteristics of a motivated manager.

What Is Motivation?

It's difficult to motivate others unless you're already motivated yourself. Motivation is the drive to do well, to succeed, to please, to perform. Are you motivated to do the best job you can? Are you enthused about going to your job each day? When employees, managers and owners are excited about their work, outstanding performance will follow.

Motivation and self-esteem are closely interrelated. Motivated employees feel good about themselves. People with high self-esteem naturally do a better job.

How Motivated Are You?

Do you consider yourself highly motivated, or is your enthusiasm beginning to slip? Do you know how to protect and bolster your self-esteem, or do you become easily upset and defensive when your work is being criticized?

If you've been doing the same job for a period of time with little reward, recognition or promotion, chances are your sense of motivation is slipping. No need to despair. The real problem might be with your company.

Look around and try to determine how your company motivates its top-level managers and supervisors. If your boss doesn't take an active part in helping you get promoted, recognize your achievements, or hand you a bonus for a job well done, then it's difficult for you to pass on a sense of passion and commitment to your staff.

Internal vs. External Motivation

Occasionally, an uninspired department can pull together and accomplish miracles. It's usually a crisis situation that requires employees to pit themselves against unbeatable odds and win. Working toward a specifically defined short-term goal in a crisis situation is considered external motivation. The results can be spectacular. Employees who formerly approached their work with a lackluster spirit can surprise the most seasoned manager with their innovation and creativity. Likewise, a somewhat uninspired manager can be transformed into an inspired group leader by the dynamics of external motivators. As one business expert said, "By nature, people are interested in doing well, in being effective workers and effective achievers."

External motivators work because:

1. They allow group work habits to change and become more creative and productive.

2. They allow individuals to discover and develop their hidden talents through brainstorming, work planning and dynamic communication.

3. The group learns to play as a team, to pull together toward a common goal and to win.

4. Individuals learn to value themselves as part of a productive, innovative group.

5. When external motivators involve bonuses, incentives or recognition, individuals feel honored and duly compensated.

Unfortunately, external motivators have a limited life span. Their effectiveness usually lasts only the length of the project or however long it takes to achieve the specified goal. When the carrot is taken away, a highly motivated department can easily slip back into low productivity. External motivators work like sugar in the bloodstream. They can produce short bursts of high energy, good for achieving short-term goals, but lack the sustaining power of internal motivators for more long-term efforts.

When external motivators are based exclusively on financial rewards, they can be interpreted as coercion. This breeds frustration and resentment among employees.

In the long run, internal motivators work better than external motivators because they build upon a psychological structure already in place — self-esteem.

Employees need to know that their company cares about them. Effective managers are able to communicate that caring, but to do so they must genuinely care about themselves. Self-esteem is the hidden ingredient in a motivated leader's formula for success.

To determine your level of self-esteem, consider the following questions:

1. Do you continually compare yourself to others and feel you don't measure up? If so, you need to understand that everyone is different and possesses diverse talents and abilities. Learn to value your own abilities, opportunities and achievements as unique.

2. Do you reward yourself for a job well done? If not, get into the habit of rewarding yourself. Try dinner at a favorite restaurant or going to a movie with a friend. Also, concentrate on internal rewards; give yourself a pat on the back and bask in the glow of meeting a goal.

3. Do you accept praise well or does it make you feel uncomfortable? If you're uncomfortable, become aware of your body language. Practice looking your colleague in the eye and saying, "Thank you. I worked hard on that project. Your appreciation means a lot to me." Let it sink in. Hear praise while it's being given. Replay it to yourself afterward.

4. Do you accept what's positive about yourself? If not, get reinforcement for your positive attributes from friends and colleagues. Don't dwell on past mistakes. View problems as opportunities to learn.

5. Do you indulge in self-criticism? If so, reinforce your self-confidence with positive imagery and affirmations. "I can handle this easily. Managing this project is fulfilling and fun for me." Disconnect yourself from negative inner voices. Become your own cheerleader. Be objective. Ask yourself, "Is this criticism justified? Does it serve a positive purpose?" If not, get rid of it.

Internal motivation pays off in the long run because it's not dependent on the artificial structure of meeting a deadline, satisfying a quota, or topping a departmental sales record. When you're motivated from within, your employees trust you for your consistency. They see that there's no slacking off as certain goals are met and commitment to high quality is permanent.

Internal motivation helps differentiate the stars from the fair-to-mediocre workers.

These top performers' internal motivation has helped them to develop and sustain qualities essential to business success.

- Initiative: Going above and beyond standard job expectations. Solving problems. Improving processes.

- Drive: The pursuit of excellence. Doing a good job because they want to, not because someone is watching.

- Leadership: Challenging others to solve their own problems and inspiring others to high levels of performance. Setting the pace by example.

- Flexibility: Adapting to the perpetually changing business environment. Dealing effectively with various personality types and work styles.

Mission Statements — Does Yours Match Your Company's?

Your company has a mission statement. Do you? It's important to know why you're working and what you're trying to achieve, both on a personal and managerial level.

A mission statement is not an action plan. Action plans are specific steps with measurable results that will help you achieve your predefined goals. For instance, your five-year action plan might look something like this:

1. Boost next year's departmental production by 20 percent. Decrease turnover 25 percent by incorporating stronger team building.

2. Increase lateral networking. Offer my department's services to help test Research and Development's ideas. In turn, initiate brainstorming in R & D that can benefit marketing.

3. Use interdepartmental support and documentation to ask my boss for a promotion to vice president.

Mission statements are much simpler than action plans. Your company's mission statement tells why and for what purpose the organization was formed; what services, goods and ideas it offers the public; and what its standards are.

Your mission statement may be short-term or project-related. If so, chances are you're more involved in putting out fires than in seeing the big picture. You're reacting to external stimuli rather than focusing on internal beliefs and values.

Your mission statement should reflect what you really want to do with your life. Commitment to a personal mission is the cornerstone on which high performers build their success. What is your greatest desire? What do you hope to achieve by working for the company that employs you? See if any of these answers fit you:

1. To become the first woman vice president.

2. To do the best job I can, to listen to my employees attentively, to let them know I care.

3. To have a hand in guiding my company's development from a small manufacturer to an international corporation.

4. To grow with this company, both psychologically and technically. To meet the demands of effective managing with clarity and purpose. To develop expertise.

Write down your personal mission statement. Realistically assess whether you can achieve what you want in your current job. See whether your personal mission statement and your company's mission statement are in sync. A good blend of the two will allow you to:

1. Organize your experience around a single unifying theme.

2. Seek and find a purpose.

3. Feel proud of yourself.

4. Achieve goals.

5. Make a contribution.

6. Follow your action plans purposefully and tenaciously.

One common demotivator for talented managers is being stuck in the wrong company. Certain kinds of work environments and corporate policies can actually alienate enthusiastic performers. Ask yourself whether your company places any of these unnecessary obstacles in your path:

1. Citing historical precedent. "This is the way we have always done things in the past." Most businesses know by now that this non-innovative attitude is the quickest way to the corporate graveyard. It favors rigidity and outmoded practices over creativity and new information.

2. Bad supervision. The company employs managers who give orders without explanation. They're impatient with subordinates who complain of boredom, pointless work and lack of opportunity. This attitude is adversarial and counterproductive. Instead of listening to employees and seeking ways to address their complaints, managers view employees as unmotivated and lazy. Employees, on the other hand, view their managers as callous and indifferent.

3. Bureaucratic organizational structure. By its very nature, bureaucracy does not foster good communication (the boss talks, the employee listens). The organization's over-involvement with

red tape, meaningless details and policies frustrates any attempts to make positive changes. Employees feel they are of no consequence to the managers above them in the bureaucratic hierarchy.

Your ability to make changes in the above scenarios depends on your rank, position and how much power you actually wield. Companies in trouble, with sliding sales figures and poor morale may be willing to listen. You can introduce new management concepts based on:

1. Participatory management. Managers seldom make unilateral decisions, preferring to increase employee involvement in a work climate that is reward-centered.

2. Management by objectives. Managers explain to workers the results they expect, then allow workers to decide how to achieve those ends by prioritizing tasks and measuring their own performance.

3. Quality circles. Managers recognize workers as experts by organizing a small group of employees in the same work area who have been trained to identify and analyze problems related to their own jobs.

Depending on your level of motivation and commitment, you can offer your own department as a pioneer group to put these management theories into practice. Do your homework, however. Before making such a proposal:

1. Poll your employees; find out whether they'll support your decision. Discuss your ideas openly with those who oppose them.

2. Find out how much time it will take for these management practices to get results. Talk to managers in other companies who have adopted more flexible approaches. Give yourself a realistic time frame in which your efforts can mature.

3. Make sure your company is behind you and that you aren't being set up to fail. If necessary, get written statements of support. Make sure other departments can't sabotage your work.

Even if your company decides not to adopt your management techniques, you'll have the satisfaction of developing better work relationships with your employees. On the other hand, if your proposal is accepted, you will have the external motivator of being in the company spotlight. Your employees will perform better, work harder and become better team players.

What Are the Characteristics of a Motivated Manager?

To determine how motivated you are, look at how well you motivate others. Ask yourself how well you've incorporated the following skills into your own management style. A motivated manager:

1. Is totally committed to the job.

2. Hires the best people. The success of your leadership is represented by the quality of people with whom you surround yourself.

3. Recognizes employees' strengths and talents. Just as no two snowflakes are alike, no two people are alike. Different employees have different abilities. Maybe you're not aware that your rather mediocre word-processing technician has outstanding accounting abilities. Watch. Listen. Be on the lookout for talented, ambitious employees who take classes to hone their skills and who ask for additional training.

4. Helps employees recognize and appreciate their own abilities. Avoid letting your employees become competitive with one another, comparing skills, income, lifestyles, etc. Listen to and nurture each employee separately. Help your employees uncover and develop their special gifts.

5. Doesn't ignore weaknesses, but doesn't dwell on them, either. Help your employees recognize and correct their own weaknesses. Be positive, diplomatic and open-minded.

6. Does not treat subordinates like children. Don't manipulate employees, order them about or tell them what they must do. Encourage them to take the initiative for improving their performance. Help them understand the value of playing by the rules.

7. Is an energetic team player. If you are not an active team member, how can you expect others who may have less of a stake in the success of the project to be active? Encourage team spirit by putting the success of the team ahead of personal advancement and recognition.

8. Takes the heat when necessary rather than passing the buck. Admit your mistakes. If others are partly responsible, discuss it with them individually and privately.

9. Assesses the best way to deal with each situation. No two employees are alike. No two employees will react the same way to criticism, counseling or reprimands. Don't be too docile or conciliatory. When the situation demands it, take control.

10. Focuses on correcting employees' problem behaviors, not on their personalities. Never undermine an employee's ego or self-esteem. Follow the golden rule of management: When administering praise, do it publicly. Avoid public and thoughtless criticism of co-workers, whether subordinates or superiors.

11. Looks for solutions to problems rather than blame. Enlist employees' cooperation in problem solving. Try to depersonalize the mistakes that have caused the problem. Avoid the negatives of office politics.

12. Is honest, trustworthy and straightforward. When you make mistakes, admit them. Trust is the foundation of team spirit. Employees need to know they can trust their bosses to deal with them honestly.

13. Leads by example. Don't just talk the talk — walk the walk.

Basically, management experts say everyone wants to do well. Workers are already motivated; managers just have to remove the obstacles.

To ensure your own peak performance, it's important to realize that high achievers are no different than you or your employees. They're not people with a mysterious "X" factor added. They're people with very little of their potential taken away.

To be a motivated performer, do two things:

- Develop within yourself an ability to achieve what you set out to do.

- Cultivate within yourself the characteristics you value most.

Key Points

- A manager's level of motivation can dramatically impact the motivation of the entire group.

- Both internal and external motivators are needed for peak performance. Internal motivators are more permanent elements that workers can build their careers upon.

- Ideally, your job should allow you to work toward fulfillment of your personal mission statement.

- Common obstacles to a manager's motivation are:

    — "The way it's always been done."

    — Poor upper management.

    — Bureaucracy.

- Motivated managers who want to motivate their subordinates must lead by example and have strong, respectful and open relationships with them. Employees need to know that their managers are honest and trustworthy. They need to know that their managers care about them. That's the tough part of motivation. The rest is knowing successful techniques.

Assess your current level of motivation.

1. How long have you held your present job?

2. How have your job duties changed over the last three years? The last year?

3. Do you have more responsibilities than when you started?

4. Are you overloaded with work?

5. Does the nature of your job cause you to interact frequently with other departmental managers?

6. Can you see a progression from where you were three years ago to where you want to go within the company? Do you have an action plan?

7. Are you excited by what you do or are you a little bored?

8. Is your job fun?

How does your company motivate its top-level managers and supervisors?

1. Is the CEO a motivated, charismatic leader?

2. Does she imbue projects with a sense of excitement and purpose?

3. Do her attitudes filter down the management hierarchy and inspire her subordinates?

4. Does your immediate supervisor take responsibility for motivating you?

5. When you make suggestions, does your boss listen?

Reflections

Assess your self-esteem.

1. Do I continually compare myself to others and feel I don't measure up?

2. Do I reward myself for a job well done?

3. Do I accept praise well or does it make me feel uncomfortable?

4. Do I accept what's positive about myself?

5. Do I indulge in self-criticism?

What is your mission statement? What is the organization's mission statement? How well do they fit together? Does your present position allow you to move toward fulfilling your personal goals?

Review the characteristics of a motivated manager on pages 17 and 18. How many of them do you currently have? Which areas could use some improvement? Which one will be first?

Reflections

3 ENHANCING PERFORMANCE: MOTIVATING THROUGH TEAM BUILDING

It's an old adage that two heads are better than one for solving problems. No matter how gifted the individual player, he can accomplish a great deal more if he is part of a dedicated team.

Team building is an effective motivational device that creates a group identity. Since teamwork is an integral part of corporate life, you need to understand how it works. In this chapter, we'll look at:

- Why team play works in corporations.

- What team-building skills you, as a manager, need to develop.

- How to keep your team in the game.

Why Team Play Works in Corporations

As children, nearly all of us experienced the thrill of victory, whether playing softball, high-school volleyball or neighborhood basketball. We all remember basking in the warm glow of winning and learning to value ourselves and our teammates for the special combination of talents and abilities that made us winners. People exposed to team play in sports at an early age learn invaluable lessons that can later be applied to corporate life. They are:

1. Know the game plan. The goal is to win the game. A good coach has a strategy for winning. Every team is different; therefore, every game that pits one team against another is different. Know your

team's strengths and weaknesses. Know your opponents' strengths and weaknesses. Figure out how your team can maximize its strengths against the opposition.

2. Know the rules and play by them. A good coach teaches his team the rules and insists on fair play. The team that doesn't abide by the rules will be penalized. A good player doesn't limit himself to learning only the rules that apply to his position. He also learns the rules that govern the overall game as well as those specific to each player's position. This approach gives the team flexibility: the ability of one player to play any position.

3. Know your position and how to play it. A structured, organized team functions in the same manner as any other well-defined social unit. Depending on his innate talents or experience, each player occupies a certain position on the team. With that position come certain responsibilities. A player knows how his duties fit into the overall operation of the team. When he is well-motivated, a player performs to the best of his ability, is a credit to the team and ensures its success. Personal glory and recognition are secondary to the good of the team.

4. It takes all types to make a team. Not all players are equally good at the same endeavors. Some are fast runners, some are strong hitters, some are great pitchers. Some teammates are good guys, some are bad guys, some are extremely capable, some have fewer skills to contribute to the team effort. Nevertheless, individual members must adjust to one another and learn to play together as a team. Divisiveness among teammates is not allowed. It's simply bad sportsmanship.

5. Don't question the coach's decisions. Every team needs a leader, a decision maker, an arbiter. The coach is the ultimate authority and motivator. Although team members may not always agree with the coach's decisions, they are obligated to implement them. All players participate in the planning sessions, but the coach makes the final decision in planning strategy and dictating plays.

6. Learn from losing. The best games are played between two evenly matched opponents. It's no fun when teams are grossly mismatched in terms of their abilities. When both teams are playing their best, there's no dishonor in losing. Learning how to lose gracefully becomes part of the bigger game plan. If the possibility of losing didn't exist, there would be no sense in trying to win and no motivation to improve. Teams learn to take defeat in stride. They learn to treat failure as a revitalizing force. Losing a game signals the need for more practice, better techniques and improved team coordination.

Key Functions of the Team

Although each team within each corporation is a unique entity, all successful teams perform eight key functions. They are:

- Information processing. Finding out what others are doing, ensuring the team is following the best practices, and ensuring the team has all the information available to make its best decisions and deliver results.

- Innovating. Challenging the way things are currently being done. There are always better ways of doing things if one only takes time to discover them.

- Persuading/influencing. Obtaining the resources the team needs can only be accomplished by convincing others that they are necessary.

- Developing. Matching ideas to the needs of customers, clients or users; listening to them and incorporating requests into your plans as permitted by the resource constraints of your organization.

- Structuring. Organizing the team so that everyone knows what they have to do, how they have to do it and when, so that results are delivered on time and within budget.

- Producing. Delivering the product or service.

- Assessing/integrating. Self-auditing for errors and upholding standards to maintain effective work processes.

- Coordinating. Ensuring that all team members pull together.

Basic Team-Building Skills

Obviously, not everyone on your team of corporate players has had exposure to the concepts outlined above. You might even be feeling somewhat intimidated by your own lack of experience in unifying and motivating a diverse group of people.

It's simpler than it sounds. As a manager/coach, you need to keep in mind four basic strategies that can help you incorporate team building:

1. Perceive the goal.

2. Devise a strategy so you can reach it.

3. Motivate the team to do it.

4. Prepare to overcome obstacles that stand in your way.

Goal setting is the first major element in team building. It unifies team members by giving them a shared sense of mission or objective. The second element in team building is communicating that goal to your team.

To set goals effectively, you must have a clear idea of what they are. Whatever the goal, make sure you share the game plan with your staff. Don't simply dictate your wishes — make your staff members feel that their involvement is important and they are part of the process. Show them why they're critical to the project's outcome and why you're proud to have them on your team by communicating:

1. Why the goal is important.

2. Why their involvement is critical.

3. How they will benefit from its success.

Why the Goal Is Important

It's hard for team members to pull together to reach a common goal unless they understand why that goal is important. Following are some strategies that can help you reiterate the importance of what your team is doing.

- Be enthusiastic. Share your sense of mission and enthusiasm with team members. Communicate not only your excitement, but also the significance of what the team is doing, why it matters to the company and what the outcome means for the team.

- Be specific. Don't generalize with comments like, "As part of Research and Development, we're going to come up with the best ideas this company has ever had." Instead, make your objectives concrete and achievable: "To increase sales, this department needs to improve the product we offer our customers. Here's how we're going to structure a new pilot program, and here's the percentage of market turnaround we're shooting for." Come to every team meeting with information that reflects the team's accomplishments. Convey a sense of activity and accomplishment through visual aids, reports, and feedback from individuals to whom you've assigned duties.

- Be informative. Share information and be thorough. Give team members the history of the project; tell them its background, why it's a priority, and who made what decisions. Let them know what impact the project will have on the company as a whole.

- Be realistic. To motivate effectively, the goal must be clear and attainable. If possible, state each goal in terms of what the employee must contribute instead of merely forecasting the outcome. You might achieve your best results by explaining the goal, then allowing each team member to identify his contribution within given parameters. Let each team member set specific targets.

- Be flexible. Realize that the goal may change as your team works through the process of achieving it. Be willing to change as the goal changes. Keep communications clear and open.

Show Your Team Members Why Their Involvement Is Critical

Team building is one of the best ways to encourage employees to motivate themselves and one another. Consistently conveying that the company cares about them is one of the most effective ways to inspire their self-motivation. You can communicate that you and the company care by following these practices:

- Know your players and their individual goals. Before tackling the first big kickoff meeting, do a little investigating. Talk to each individual who will be playing on your team. Find out what motivates him. Explain how the team's success will meet each person's individual goals.

- Give them permission to be participating members of the team.

- Include, don't exclude. You need strong team members who feel they're a vital part of the group. When people feel important and included, you motivate them. Create a team atmosphere that welcomes outsiders, is embracing and nurturing. The motivation that stems from inclusion builds bridges between individuals and builds the group as a whole. Exclusion, which occurs when petty rivalries and negativity exist, builds walls.

- Create opportunities for them to express their thoughts, ideas and opinions.

- Value the individual. Let team members know that you value each person for his individual talents and abilities. Discourage competitiveness among players. Encourage innovation and creativity by conducting brainstorming sessions where there are no wrong answers. Develop and maintain your sense of humor.

- Encourage them to listen and give feedback to one another.

Communicate the Benefits of Success

Whenever possible, reiterate how team members will benefit from the project's success. Be careful how you do it. Sell, don't tell. As manager, your job is to persuade, not to order.

- Rewards that motivate. If a successful outcome includes a cash bonus or a Caribbean cruise, use the reward as part of your motivation strategy. Effective rewards include recognition (an awards banquet), promotions, and affirmations of individuals' efforts from other managers in the company.

- Benefits of being on the team. It's possible that some of your team members have never played on a team before, much less a winning team. Stress the benefits of teamwork. By project's end, everyone on your team will have demonstrated his ability to take on additional responsibilities, meet goals and motivate one another.

- Emphasize training. Team members can derive benefits if they are asked to cross-train by learning other team members' jobs. They may also be guinea pigs in product research as the first to test new software or managerial methods, or sell new products. Convey to your team members that these firsts put them on the cutting edge in their industry and give them a wider spectrum of skills and abilities, and, thus, a better chance at future promotions.

How to Keep Your Team in the Game

You've got your team assembled and everyone seems eager and willing to work together. A week later, it's a different story. Some players are apathetic, others are confused, and some are downright hostile toward you and one another. They feel the time spent on the team is jeopardizing their "real jobs." What do you do?

1. Define roles. This should be your first step. If you already did it, then redefine roles. You may have to do this at each team meeting by asking for progress reports that are identified with team positions. Reiterate with comments like, "Maloney, as I recall, you're in charge of our database management. Would you like to fill us in on where your retrieval system stands?"

   You can avoid power struggles by documenting each person's responsibilities and authority within the group. When there are questions, check the notes of the appropriate meeting. Follow up meetings with memos that outline decisions and action plans. Make sure each team member is on the distribution list. Ask for comments on the memos at the next meeting.

2. Draw up a game plan. Players need to know what's expected of them in advance. Each player must understand what he needs to do and what everyone else needs to do to reach the goal. If you feel there's some confusion, ask players to reiterate their responsibilities: who they communicate with, which players they're in charge of, who they need approval from to go ahead, and so on.

3. Create an identity for the team. Give your team a name that makes its players proud. Call it the "Task Force for Research and Development." Let the team name itself. Put an item in the company newsletter that explains why the team has been created and what its goals are. Discuss the team and its mission in departmental meetings, and mention players and their positions by name. Your team members will feel connected to the rest of the

company, and feel important and recognized. Giving your team an identity helps individual players become visible. That feeling of being in the spotlight helps to ensure cooperation among team members.

4. Be willing to reassign positions. A good manager gives the right job to the right person at the right time. Observe your players; find out which ones are your "people people" and which are your "paper people." The former are better at interacting with others, usually possessing highly developed verbal skills. The latter are "techies," who are more interested in working with technology, concepts and ideas. "People people" excel in the following positions: customer service, negotiation, training, presentations and supervision. "Paper people" are good at research and analysis, design, technical writing, operations and troubleshooting. You might want to switch a team member to another position if he is not suited to his current one.

5. Give your players a chance to stretch their skills. When an employee is playing his position too easily, you might want to switch him to a more difficult position. Use assignments as rewards for top performers and you'll get better results.

6. Encourage networking. Give players the freedom to stay in frequent contact and exchange information with each other. At your first meeting, establish how the team will communicate (through correspondence, memos, bulletin boards, electronic mail, etc.) and how often. Make sure team members know how to reach each other after hours, and who has authority to make decisions when you're not available.

7. Reinforce the team concept at every opportunity. When the group has done well, praise the entire group. Don't praise individuals before the group. If an individual team member has performed in an outstanding manner that you want to recognize, take him aside and praise him privately.

The key to establishing and maintaining good teamwork is to create a caring atmosphere. If employees believe their manager, and hence their company, truly cares about them, high performance naturally follows. To communicate this, you must demonstrate:

- A sense of excitement and commitment to the team's defined goal.

- An appreciation and support for the team as a unit and for individual team members.

Improving Performance Through Teams

1. Specify the values and behaviors emphasized and desired by the team.

2. Assess the typical leadership roles in the team.

3. Identify skill areas that each team member could enhance.

4. Identify which decisions are to be made by which team members.

5. Communicate the plan for effective information flow within and outside the team.

6. Establish the ground rules for constructive feedback among team members.

7. Specify the process through which a team member's problem behavior is to be addressed.

8. Determine how the team is to be held accountable for results.

9. Establish an auditing process of team development and performance.

10. Identify how individuals on the team are motivated and how each is to be recognized for his accomplishments.

Key Points

- In this chapter we've looked at how teams work at the corporate level. We have examined some of the basics that every team member learns as a child and have applied them to the workplace.

- Know the game plan and be able to communicate it to your team. Capitalize on team members' strengths to reach the goal. Figure out the rules and how to play by them. The better your players understand the rules, the better they'll be able to cover their own and other players' positions.

- One of the most important team-building skills you can have as a manager is the ability to communicate why the goal is important. You can do this by being enthusiastic, specific and informative.

- Show your team members why their involvement is critical. Explain to each individual how the team's success can help realize individual goals.

- Once your team is in the game, maintain motivation by keeping roles defined, having a clear game plan, and giving the team an identity.

- If you run into trouble, don't be afraid to reassign positions that will give your players a chance to stretch their skills.

1. What does your company hope to accomplish through teams?

2. What is your company's philosophy regarding teams? Where's the primary focus: on simplifying work and improving processes? On motivating employees?

3. How effective is your team communication? Are individuals uncomfortable asking for feedback, for fear that it may be negative?

4. Do you feel uncomfortable relinquishing any responsibility to the group?

5. Do you usually reward individuals for performance, rather than the group as a whole?

6. Rate your team's effectiveness in each of the functions of a team.

	Very effective	Reasonably effective	Could use improvement	Really needs work
Information processing				
Innovating				
Persuading/influencing				
Developing				
Structuring				
Producing				
Assessing/integrating				
Coordinating				

Reflections

4 IMPROVING PERFORMANCE: MOTIVATING THROUGH DELEGATION

Delegation is one of the most successful means a manager has to increase teamwork. When handled properly, it's a way to improve the abilities of your employees, build their confidence, and encourage them to take risks. In addition, top managers use delegation as a way to enhance their own strengths.

To delegate well, however, managers must perform a delicate balancing act by juggling their employees' needs for greater autonomy with their own needs to remain in control. Delegation is not as simple as it sounds. It can be a big demotivator when employees feel that their eagerness to prove themselves has been exploited by callous management, or if they equate delegation with manipulation by company bosses.

Ideally, however, delegation can be your means to hone a team of top performers. It can free you of time-consuming management details and make you a better leader.

In this chapter, we'll show you the secrets of effective delegation by examining:

- What delegation does.

- When to delegate.

- Ways to delegate effectively.

What Delegation Does

It's the job of management to accomplish organizational goals through the efforts of others. To be effective in reaching goals, managers must have the confidence to delegate responsibility and authority to their employees. The more your staff can achieve, the more successful your entire company can be. Therefore, delegation benefits both bosses and their subordinates by:

- Freeing up a manager's time so she can be a more effective leader.

- Empowering employees by giving them greater autonomy and responsibility.

- Promoting teamwork between management and workers by creating an open atmosphere of trust.

The concept of delegation is undergoing continuous change. Historically, it meant assigning various tasks and responsibilities to one's employees. A more enlightened approach is for management to delegate by removing obstacles so that employees are freer to do their jobs. Whatever your approach to delegation, it's important to know some basic do's and don'ts.

1. Do use your authority to delegate. If you don't use your authority, you lose it.

2. Do delegate the necessary authority when you delegate responsibility.

3. Do delegate only to employees who you are confident can handle the authority.

4. Do clearly define the responsibilities delegated to each subordinate.

5. Do follow up to be sure the job is getting done, but avoid micromanagement.

6. Do provide a road map with clear and specific targets, so employees are comfortable acting on their own.

7. Do back up the employee you've delegated work to with your support.

8. Do set up a formal, ongoing progress-reporting system.

9. Do be clear with each subordinate about what decisions she can make.

10. Do focus on results rather than process.

11. Do clearly state deadlines and priorities.

12. Do find each employee's talents and utilize them.

13. Do help your employees shine.

On the other hand ...

1. Don't interfere unnecessarily with the work you've delegated.

2. Don't use delegation as a way to dump your duties on subordinates. Its purpose is to provide you with an increased capacity for greater responsibility.

3. Don't delegate in such a way that your employee ends up with "dual supervision" — accountable to more than one boss.

4. Don't solve all the problems. Teach your employees to solve the problems themselves.

When to Delegate

Scenario A:

A bright, young CEO of her own athletic footwear company found that rapid growth brought as many problems as rewards. In less than two years, sales had climbed from zero to $16 million. The final battle of priorities occurred during the planning session for the annual trade show. The CEO had to make a difficult decision. Should she oversee the myriad of details for the show, which was important to maintain her company's sales, or should she spend the time interviewing retailers? "I just couldn't do everything myself. I knew that if I didn't delegate, some area in my company would suffer," she recalled. Literally forced to delegate, the CEO chose to let her public relations manager handle the planning of the trade show. The results? "Orders exceeded our expectations."

How does this CEO feel about her choice to delegate? "Good. Employees need guidance and freedom to do their jobs right."

Scenario B:

The president of a company that provides tour services and sells more than 650,000 leis annually to tourists in Hawaii began having trouble managing the business she founded in 1972. Her operations grew to employ 1,000 people, yet she was managing them the same way she did when there were just 100 employees. "I was functioning as a dictator," the president recalled. "I was reaching the point where I could not do everything on my own. I had to release some of the authority and responsibility."

Luckily, one of her vice presidents encouraged her to attend a series of management courses that stressed the need for clear communication of objectives and delegation. Taking these principles to heart, the president began actively delegating responsibilities and communicating goals and objectives to everyone in the organization. Before, she said, the chain of command was very unclear. It made delegation very difficult. Now each employee is introduced to all other facets of the business, as well as organizational charts. "We learned that you cannot delegate successfully and expect an employee to function at her optimum unless the manager has been successful in conveying the big picture to her."

In both scenarios, knowing when to delegate was half the battle. Ideally, managers have highly motivated, talented staff members all primed and ready to jump into a demanding project designed just for them. But it seldom works that way in real life.

Unfortunately, delegation is often a panicked response to a crisis situation or in response to outside pressures, such as:

- When an unexpected growth spurt has strained your company's resources to maximum capacity.

- When your company has developed and diversified over a period of time, yet business is still being conducted as if the company were much smaller.

- When your job, because of added responsibilities and deadlines, has become unmanageable.

- When your talented subordinates are bored and underutilized, making them ripe candidates for divisiveness and political infighting.

Ideally, managers should only delegate to employees whom they have confidence in. It's important to remember that delegation can often turn an unmotivated, troublesome employee into a high achiever and solid team player.

Good managers don't wait until a situation is beyond their control to delegate. Knowing *when* to delegate is as important as knowing *what* to delegate. Begin delegating when:

1. You or a staff member are overloaded. Delegation is not a permanent reassignment of work and duties, but a temporary redistribution.

2. An employee would benefit from the experience of having her abilities tested by a new assignment. The delegated work could help prepare a promising employee for a future promotion by allowing her to demonstrate new skills.

3. You can monitor the outcome of the work. Never delegate when you have no means of reviewing and approving work methods and results. Should the employee be unable to handle the delegated work, have an alternative solution available.

4. It's an assignment you would like to do, but can't. Never dump unwanted tasks on employees. They'll resent the assignment and you.

Ways to Delegate

In many organizations, delegation is a haphazard process. A conversation or note between two individuals results in the delegation of a task. Chances are that the communication does not include the necessary information for the delegation to be effective.

Effective delegation requires the communication to be carefully planned based upon the complexity and priority of the specific task in question. At the conclusion of the communication, the person taking on the assignment must have all the information necessary to act and make decisions for success. She should be motivated, directed and obligated.

Delegation does not mean simply asking an employee to complete a list of tasks. The problem with that approach is that the employee is placed in a bind: She must carry out responsibilities without having the ability to make decisions on how the tasks should be done. Managers who pay lip service to delegation, but secretly hang onto control, are doing their staff a grave disservice. Delegation without control is a big demotivator.

Delegation means giving a subordinate enough authority to complete the task. Managers must consider their employees' individual capabilities and then provide them with whatever authority is required to fulfill the assigned responsibilities. An acceptable method of checking on an employee's progress must also be established.

1. Determine the type of work to be delegated.

2. Identify desired results and provide examples of success. Expectations must be clearly stated if they are to be met.

3. Assign responsibility. When you delegate, be sure to convey responsibility. Make sure the employee understands that the task

she has been assigned is important to you, and that you have confidence in her ability to complete it successfully.

4. Provide authority and support. Make the limits of her authority clear to the employee. Provide her with support by explaining her authority to her peers. Make sure she understands she is not to abuse her authority. Remember that delegating with limited authority (your continual checking to see if everything is running smoothly) contradicts the purpose of delegation.

5. Obtain commitment and agreement.

6. Hold the employee responsible for the outcome. Make it clear that delegation is a vote of confidence in your employee's ability to meet goals. Provide her with checkpoints at consistent, predetermined times. For instance, you can keep tabs on operations through weekly checkup meetings.

7. Reward results.

Problems in Delegating

Occasionally delegation causes, rather than solves, problems. Delegation involves a certain amount of risk. Good managers have carefully calculated their odds of success and failure, and know what a failure will cost them. By delegating, a manager chooses to turn over work she knows she can do but lacks time for, to an employee she assumes can do the work. When problems arise, it's because managers have misjudged the demands of the assignment or the ability of the employee. Here are some common problems and steps managers can take to avoid them:

1. The employee to whom you've delegated responsibility starts to slack off, procrastinates and fails to meet deadlines. At this point you should call a meeting, define the problem and develop alternatives. Try to avoid taking the project away from the employee, if possible; sometimes it may be your only solution.

Other options include:

- When the problem is technical, assign a staff expert to advise the employee.

- When the problem is a lack of motivation, assign a coach to the employee to help her through the rough spots.

2. The deadline on the project you've delegated is suddenly shortened. However, your employee requires more than the available time to finish it. In this case, get feedback from your employee. Explain how the deadline has changed. Seek ideas from her on how the deadline can be met. Give her the option of sticking with the project. Offer her expert help and round-the-clock guidance. Come to a solution that is mutually satisfactory so your employee doesn't feel pressured to (a) finish a highly pressured project, or (b) abandon a rewarding project midway to completion.

Finally, once you've delegated, stay out of the way. Managers who are too controlling don't allow employees the autonomy to get involved and structure their own work. Overly controlling managers may think they're delegating, but in reality they are secretly threatened by employees being in charge of their own work. The controlling manager wants employees to do it her way. The outcome is a gradual slowdown of productivity and diminishing of morale.

Take it from savvy delegators who say that management's job is to remove the obstacles so employees can get in there and do their jobs.

Key Points

- Delegation benefits both bosses and subordinates in three ways:

    1. It frees up managers to take on more leadership responsibilities.

    2. It empowers subordinates.

    3. It promotes teamwork between management and staff.

- Delegation often occurs at the least opportune moment. But it can be used effectively to stave off crises brought about by:

  1. Rapid company expansion.

  2. Resistance of a company to management planning.

  3. Underutilization of talented staff.

- Good managers know it's appropriate to delegate when:

  1. They're overloaded.

  2. The delegated responsibility would benefit an employee.

  3. They can monitor the progress of the delegated assignment.

- Managers should delegate authority as well as responsibility. With authority, an employee has greater autonomy over her own work. Avoid being over-controlling and dumping unwanted tasks. Delegate important projects.

	Yes	No

1. Do you delegate differently based on the type of work to be completed?

2. Do you carefully explain why the task needs to be done?

3. Do you clarify obstacles and limitations that will be involved?

4. Are budget constraints made clear?

5. Do you set a due date?

6. Do you establish an ongoing feedback loop?

7. Do you take supportive, rather than directive, action if progress is not satisfactory?

8. Do you clearly state what the limits of authority are?

9. Do you provide examples of success?

10. Are the rewards specified?

11. Are employees enthusiastic to take on new delegated work from you?

Reflections

5 ENHANCING PERFORMANCE: MOTIVATING THROUGH COMMUNICATION

Ask any good manager, and he will likely tell you that communication skills are among the most important sources of personal power. Being able to convey the big picture to one's employees is a major motivational tool. Yet, many managers do not realize that *how* they communicate is just as important as *what* they communicate.

Along with the concept of team play as a means of building organizational unity is the need to communicate more effectively. Enlightened managers no longer shout orders and yell at employees who disobey them. They realize communication is a means by which they can solicit employees' opinions to shape objectives. When it comes to being managed, employees don't resist their own ideas.

Communication requires well-developed listening skills. As the president of a successful computer manufacturing company has said: "In this organization we listen more than we talk, because we think that is the best way to learn."

In this chapter we'll look at various aspects of good communication and how it keeps your staff motivated:

- What makes people want to listen to you.

- What to communicate.

- How to communicate.

- Meetings that motivate.

- How to listen well.

What Makes People Want to Listen to You?

We've all had the uncomfortable experience of being in an audience, shifting restlessly in our seats while a speaker drones away behind a podium. He might even be discussing a subject we're actually interested in, yet something about his manner or style of presentation is boring.

We've also had the reverse experience. We've listened raptly and attentively, practically on the edge of our chairs, as a speaker mesmerizes us, shares his personal experiences with us, and energizes us with his magnetism and charm.

Charisma is the mysterious, unmeasurable substance that makes people recognize and follow leaders. Most successful communicators are gifted with a certain amount of charisma. With seemingly no effort, they're able to draw us into their web of words and make their concerns our concerns. We want to be around people who project this kind of aura. They're magnetic, they're attractive, and they're unpredictable.

Yet, a charismatic leader can lose his appeal as easily as he acquires it. What separates leaders that people want to listen to from performers who just entertain is their credibility. You might have the greatest ideas in the world, but to effectively communicate and implement them you must be, above all, credible to your employees. The purpose of your communication may be to convey information, to influence and motivate others, and to seek more information by getting others to talk. But unless your personal presence conveys authenticity, genuineness, honesty, and straightforwardness, others may not trust you to guide them.

Your credibility is based on:

- **Track record.** Your track record sums up your past performance on the job, how long you've been with the company or in your present position, how well your projects have succeeded in the past, and how well you work with your employees.

- **Enthusiasm.** Your enthusiasm for a project demonstrates to your employees your level of commitment. Genuine enthusiasm also acts as a powerful motivator to rally your staff around a challenging goal. Your enthusiasm can make a task seem fun and enjoyable, even when it means hard work. As Tommy Lasorda observed, enthusiasm is catching. "When I walk in full of enthusiasm, full of self-confidence and proud to be putting that uniform on — all of those things are contagious. That's the same attitude and atmosphere this clubhouse is going to have."

- **Being informed.** When you talk, know what you're talking about. Some people substitute opinions for facts, while others rely on outmoded theories and ideas. Make sure that when you speak, especially formally before a group, you've gathered the latest information about your subject. Nothing discredits a speaker like outdated facts and statistics.

- **Being relevant.** Some speakers communicate facts well, but never relate them to the immediate problems or concerns of the audience. If possible, raise key issues that relate to your audience. Keep your speeches succinct and on target.

- **Nonverbal cues.** Your words might be telling your staff one thing, but your nonverbal language could be telling them something else. Your credibility is reinforced by the nonverbal cues you send out based on good posture and grooming, the conviction of your handshake, making eye contact while you talk, and maintaining an orderly, efficient desk.

If your communication is positive and upbeat, then your appearance, your mannerisms, the information you relate, and your environment should send the same message. Being a credible communicator is half the battle. Credibility ensures that when you have something to say, people will listen.

Patterns of Communication

	NONASSERTIVE	ASSERTIVE	AGGRESSIVE
VERBAL	• Apologetic words • Veiled meanings • Hedging: failure to come to the point • Rambling, disconnected • At a loss for words • Failure to say what you really mean • "I mean...," "You know..." • Self-defeating • Shifts responsibility to others • Devalues self	• Statement of want • Honest statement of feelings • Objective words • Direct statements that say what you mean • "I" messages • Accepts responsibility for self • Negotiates, likes "win-win"	• "Loaded" words • Accusations • Descriptive, subjective • Superior wording • "You" messages that blame or label • Puts others down • Dictator • Gives no recognition
NONVERBAL **A. General**	• Actions instead of words, hoping someone will guess what you want • Looking as if you don't mean what you say • Nervous gestures, stress	• Attentive listening behavior • An assured manner, communicating caring and strength • Relaxed, alert	• Exaggerated show of strength • Flippant, sarcastic style • Air of superiority
B. Specific **Voice**	• Weak, hesitant, soft, sometimes wavering	• Firm, warm, well-modulated, relaxed	• Tense, shrill, loud, shaking, demanding, superior
Eyes	• Averted, downcast, teary, pleading	• Open, frank, direct • Eye contact, but not staring	• Expressionless, cold, narrowed, staring, not really "seeing" you
Stance and Posture	• Lean for support, stooped, excessive head-nodding	• Well-balanced, straight, erect, relaxed	• Hands on hips, feet apart, stiff and rigid, rude
Hands	• Fidgety, fluttery, clammy	• Relaxed motions	• Clenched, abrupt gestures, finger-pointing, fist-pounding

What to Communicate

Nothing motivates employees as much as making them feel they are part of your company's decision-making process. Successful companies are discovering that an open environment which actively solicits employee feedback and promptly acts on it is the way to get a staff emotionally invested in a company's future and committed to their jobs.

Keep the channels of communication open throughout your department by:

- Sharing the big picture. Communicate your vision to your team and reiterate it often. If employees are wrapped up in the details of a project, they may lose sight of the ultimate objective. Keep repeating the reasons you're all in this together. Give them concrete examples of the rewards: promotions, raises, company recognition, etc.

- Being generous with information. Let your employees know immediately when plans change, when problems arise, or when any other changes occur that affect them or their jobs. Defuse the effect of rumors generated by crises and catastrophes by giving your staff day-by-day updates. Don't hoard information. In return, your employees will let you in on their grapevine. You'll hear the rumors before other managers do. Remember, the object isn't to encourage or participate in employee gossip, but to maintain open communication.

- Giving praise frequently and criticism sparingly. Make sure you give your staff plenty of positive feedback. Many workers complain they only receive feedback from bosses when there's a problem. Make sure you keep your communication with staff members deliberate. Praise in public; criticize in private. These signals are closely watched by the rest of your staff.

- Encouraging employee feedback. Take time to listen to your staff. They probably possess expertise in areas you know little about. If they have suggestions for improvements, give them a fair hearing.

If you think their ideas are good, give them recognition. Actions speak louder than words. When they're on target, find a way to implement their suggestions.

How to Communicate

Making the flow of communication smooth and easy depends on your verbal and visual style. Do you couch ideas in easy-to-understand metaphors and analogies? Do you flesh out a verbal presentation with visual aids? Are you careful to avoid using demotivating, overly controlling words?

Your skill in communicating with your staff has probably improved with experience. Here are some techniques that will improve your ability to communicate effectively:

- Use metaphors and analogies to make your point. Be descriptive. Give your staff a word picture they can relate to. If you are encountering difficulties at the beginning of a project, you can soothe harassed workers by saying, "Look at this as an informational wall we're trying to break through. We're hammering away every day and it seems like we're getting nowhere. Then — POW! — one day we break through and we're on the other side."

- Use visual aids to demonstrate direction. The more specific you can be, the better. Concrete examples transform abstract concepts into readily understandable facts and figures. If your goal is to increase your department's sales by a certain percentage by year-end, put a graph on the wall in the meeting room. A picture or graph is a visual reminder of your goals. It will help guide you in making day-to-day decisions. Plot out results on a monthly basis and check the progress you've made in reaching your annual goal.

- Establish an open environment. Keep office doors open and allow employees to decorate offices and cubicles as they like, as long as it is appropriate for a work environment. Avoid showing favoritism (giving a favored employee a cubicle near a window) or reinforcing office hierarchy (by addressing clerical personnel on a first-name basis and management by surname). Put everyone on a first-name basis if appropriate.

- Establish a communications center where information of interest is to be posted for all. Employees should understand that it is their responsibility to check the information center on a regular basis to remain abreast of events. A wall near the coffeepot or in the break room are possible locations.

- Schedule regular meetings. Schedule departmental meetings at a regular time and place. Try not to change your routine or skip meetings. They don't have to be long — 15 minutes will do — but meetings are effective motivators. They tell your staff you're interested in giving and receiving information.

- Be a confidence builder, not a confidence destroyer. Don't focus on what's wrong with an employee. If he needs correction, give specific guidance gracefully. Remember, that same employee may eventually play a key position on your departmental team. His ability to perform well is undermined by your criticism. Watch how you use language to communicate.

  1. Keep your language supportive, not authoritative. Avoid using words with strong negative, judgmental overtones: "ought to," "should," "can't," "don't." This kind of language conveys to your employees that you're more of a critical parent than a manager. When praising a staff member, be sure you are neither controlling nor manipulative. Both are tactics that will demotivate employees faster than a pink slip.

  2. Praise workers for a job well done, whether it was done your way or using their own unique plan of action.

  3. "You're doing a good job, now don't screw it up" is positive feedback destroyed by the tag line. Simply leave it at

"You're doing a good job." You might add "keep it up" or "thanks." Beware of offhanded put-downs intended as humor. They're not usually very funny.

4. Be positive and supportive. Acknowledge the hard work a staff member has done. "I appreciate your carrying through on this assignment and doing it so well."

- Find the positive. When evaluating an employee's performance, begin by citing a particular skill or accomplishment, then move on to problem areas. When you conclude, again remind the employee of the positive aspects of his performance, as well as the areas that need improvement.

- Vary your communication style to fit the employee. Each employee is different. When one-on-one communication is required, be aware of how that particular employee is going to respond. Vary your communication accordingly. Ask yourself these questions: How secure is he? How well does he respond to criticism? What words should I eliminate to avoid making him defensive? How can I ensure that this encounter will be productive, not demotivating?

Meetings that Motivate

The regular departmental meeting is where your communication skills are most rigorously tested. Departmental meetings should achieve some or all of the following objectives:

- Try to address employees by name. Chat with them before and after the meeting.

- Keep employees well informed about current or future developments.

- Dispel rumor and speculation through clear and concise explanations. Ask employees what they've heard and what they think.

- Enhance your employees' visibility within the department by encouraging interaction among employees during and after meetings through open discussion.

When not infused with the proper spirit of equality, caring and inclusion, your departmental meetings can degenerate into empty rituals that squelch any sharing of information. When this happens, you can bet the real communication is going on somewhere else — probably behind your back.

Here's how to ensure a more participative meeting and to simultaneously keep it on track.

1. Hold the meeting at a time (prior to break or lunch) and in an environment that are conducive to communication. Keep it brief.

2. Prepare well in advance for even a short meeting. Have an agenda and know what your purpose is for scheduling the meeting. Make sure you achieve your purpose.

3. Take notes during the meeting so you can follow up on what was discussed with appropriate action plans.

4. Make sure that topics are work- or group-related. Departmental meetings are where you can introduce new employees, new managers assigned to other areas, new sales products, plans and anticipated changes.

5. Be honest and straightforward. Remember, you're the authority. Back up whatever you say with facts. If you don't know the answer, say so, but add, "I can find that out for you." If you make a promise, follow up on it.

6. Set aside time for discussion, but limit questions by requesting that they be held until you're through talking. Schedule no more than five or 10 minutes for questions. Offer to answer any remaining questions after the meeting on a one-on-one basis.

7. Keep your tone positive and supportive. When problems arise, they should be presented in a manner that communicates confidence:

- State the problem. Make sure everyone has heard what's being discussed. "Ted voiced his concern over how the recent oil embargo may affect our sales staff, particularly the people on the road."

- Clarify the problem. Make sure you and your staff understand the real problem being discussed. If you have any information, share it. "Am I correct in assuming, Ted, that accounting doesn't think it's feasible for us to maintain our sales staff while our country's oil supplies remain uncertain?"

- Develop alternatives. After clarifying the problem, open it up for discussion. Solicit opinions from all staff members. Just because an employee is less assertive doesn't mean his opinions are less valuable.

- Keep the meeting on track. If you feel the discussion is moving too far afield, exercise your authority as leader: "Interesting as it may be, I really don't think a political recap of Middle East history applies to this discussion."

- Summarize. When the brainstorming session has ended, summarize the suggestions made. List them all without attaching any value to them. Ask the group to choose the three strongest solutions.

- Test staff members' commitment. Ask staff for their approval to take the next step: present suggestions formally to board of directors, etc. If an innovative alternative has been offered, find out how much time individuals will commit toward its development: "Carla thinks a mail-order catalog might be a viable alternative to maintaining a sales staff. Ted and Carla, how would you feel about producing a pilot catalog? Will you take it to the next planning meeting?"

- Make the decision for taking the next step. After checking out departmental support, state the decision, backed up with an action plan. "Ted and Carla, let's get together after this meeting to target the informational needs to be presented in a catalog. Then, we'll meet a week from today and see what we've got."

Departmental meetings are ideal places for team building. They're good places to restate goals, share your vision, and give the team a collective pat on the back. Never use departmental meetings to praise or criticize individual performance.

How to Listen Well

According to management experts, listening to others' ideas is just as important, if not more so, as talking about your own ideas. Perhaps listening is difficult for you. You find yourself becoming restless and irritable when employees ramble on endlessly or are too shy and withdrawn to communicate clearly.

Being a good, motivating manager means you develop and ensure good communication with your employees. This means becoming a good listener. The key is developing empathy by putting yourself in the other guy's place. An employee can immediately sense when a boss has put his preconceived opinions on hold and is really paying attention. The employee then relaxes, opens up and talks.

Empathetic listening accomplishes the following:

1. Ensures an open flow of communication within your department. Employees know you will always give them a fair hearing.

2. Builds trust and teamwork. The more you listen to your employees, the more they'll listen to you.

3. Demonstrates your respect for the capabilities and potential contributions of others.

You can hone your listening skills by observing the interpersonal dynamics around you. Watch for the roles employees seem to adopt toward one another in departmental meetings. Observe relationships between people and between groups in the workplace. Learn to spot adversarial situations, misunderstandings and counterproductive competition between managers and employees.

The more insight you have into your employees, the better you'll be able to motivate them. Being an effective listener is an important way to gain this insight. Practice these empathetic listening skills:

1. Let the other person do the talking. This may not be easy, particularly if you and your employee aren't that well acquainted. You can stimulate discussion with remarks like, "Well, you've heard me talk for the last 10 minutes. How about telling me how you feel?"

2. Refrain from diagnosing, advising or interpreting. Don't jump to conclusions and try to figure out the problem before you have all the facts. Encourage the employee to talk. You can do this with nonverbal cues, like nodding your head, keeping eye contact and maintaining a pleasant expression.

3. Occasionally ask open-ended questions. Communication can be brought to a sudden halt if you bluntly ask a question that can be answered either "yes" or "no." Your employee starts to feel like he's being interrogated. Don't say, "Tell me, Fred, do you like your job?" Ask instead, "What three things about your job do you like the best?"

   Asking questions accomplishes many things:

   • Shows that you are listening.

   • Helps you better understand the person speaking.

- Gets the speaker back on track.

- Helps with problem solving.

- Clarifies the message.

- Satisfies your curiosity.

- Draws the other party out.

4. Practice reflective listening. Reiterate what the employee has said to demonstrate that you listened. This gives the employee feedback, yet allows you to avoid giving opinions and advice. "You're saying, Fred, that the report you submitted wasn't fairly reviewed."

5. Give information about the problem. When the employee needs feedback from you, give it. "I've been told this project is only scheduled to go until the end of the fiscal year, and then you'll be working on something entirely new."

6. Never speculate about an employee's subconscious motives. You're not Dr. Freud, and practicing amateur psychoanalysis could get you in trouble. If you're not careful, you may be projecting your own issues onto the employee. Deal with problems as the employee presents them.

7. Provide emotional support while giving approval, correction or disapproval. It's easy for employees to feel unappreciated. They want to know they did a good job and that you appreciate it. You can communicate appreciation even when you are correcting them: "First of all, Fred, I just want to tell you what fun it is having you on our team. I appreciate your innovative approach and willingness to work through the planning stage with us. I think your third-quarter projections are a little off, though. You might have to rework those."

Key Points

- It's important to remember that keeping open communication in your department is a great motivator. It depends on three things:

    1. Being credible. Having the trust and respect of your employees.

    2. Being concrete. Keeping attention focused on the actual work at hand, not slipping into generalities.

    3. Being empathetic. Identifying with your employees and knowing what makes them tick.

- The better listener you are, the better communicator you'll be. You can polish your listening skills by:

    1. Letting the other person do the talking.

    2. Refraining from diagnosing, advising or interpreting.

    3. Asking open-ended questions.

    4. Practicing reflective listening.

    5. Giving information about the problem when it's needed.

    6. Never speculating about an employee's subconscious motives.

    7. Providing emotional support while giving correction.

Communication issues	Yes	No
1. Do you feel uncomfortable asking for feedback from your team for fear that it may be negative?		
2. Do you find it difficult to treat everyone on the team equally?		
3. Do you find yourself relying on some members more than others?		
4. Do you tend to listen more to some team members than to others?		
5. Do you avoid addressing how your team members feel about some issues?		
6. Do you tend to ignore problems and hope they will resolve themselves?		
7. Do you see discussion about a problem as a waste of time?		
8. Do you dislike spending the time required for the group to achieve consensus?		
9. Do you prefer to parcel out information to the group only as required?		

Step #1 to improve your communication skills:

Reflections

What kind of listener are you?

	Never	Sometimes	Frequently	Always
1. Do you avoid deciding from the speaker's appearance whether the information is worthwhile?				
2. Do you determine your own biases and try to allow for them?				
3. Do you maintain eye contact while you listen?				
4. Do you avoid the use of status (allowing people to interrupt meetings to get your approval, signature, etc.)?				
5. Do you glance at your watch or the papers on your desk?				
6. Do you keep your mind focused on what the other person is saying?				
7. Do you interrupt when you hear an incorrect or stupid statement?				
8. Do you hear out the other person and listen to his point of view before answering?				
9. Do you make a conscious effort to evaluate the logic and credibility of what you hear?				
10. Do you avoid trying to have the last word?				

Step #1 to improve your listening skills:

6 ENHANCING PERFORMANCE: MOTIVATING THROUGH RECOGNITION

In a national business survey, employees were asked to prioritize elements of job satisfaction. The factor that repeatedly ranked first was "full appreciation of work." Job security and good wages came in fourth and fifth, respectively.

Such responses make it clear that recognition is one of the most effective motivators that managers can employ. It's also the least understood. Recognition is a way of rewarding employees for good work; unlike financial rewards, it's free. Recognition is a strong motivator because it binds an individual employee to the work group and the organizational hierarchy. In this chapter we'll look at:

- How recognition differs from financial rewards.

- Why recognition works.

- What kind of recognition works.

- When recognition doesn't work.

Recognition and Money

Recognition and money are often combined; for instance, handing out bonuses at an awards dinner. But as most managers know, the motivation provided by cash incentives has a way of wearing off. Recognition, on the other hand, forges a bond between employer and employee based on the following basic human desires:

- The need to interact with others in a meaningful way.

- The need to do good work and enjoy a sense of accomplishment.

- The need to receive recognition from a higher authority for putting forth your best effort.

How Recognition Differs from Financial Rewards

Money and recognition are the two most common ways a manager can reward employees. Even in instances when a promotion doesn't involve a salary increase, it is still an effective form of recognition by conferring upon the employee a new title, a new office and enhanced stature with the employee's peers.

As we discussed in Chapter 1, money incentives are often viewed as "job satisfiers" — factors that attract job candidates to the company. The problem with job satisfiers is that they gradually become institutionalized and their uniqueness wears off. A few decades ago it was unheard of to offer employees a wide range of benefits and profit-sharing plans. Now these "money motivators" are standard fare.

We'll discuss how money can successfully motivate employees in Chapter 7. For now, the following list shows you the common methods of reward — money and recognition — and how they differ.

Financial Rewards

Recognition Rewards

Cash

- Bonuses
- Raises
- Cash incentives
- Profit sharing
- Employee benefits

- Articles about an individual or winning team in the company newsletter
- Picture on the bulletin board of an employee shaking hands with the CEO
- Recognition at an awards banquet
- Public thanks from a higher authority at a departmental meeting

Perks

- Cruises (for top achievers)
- Paid vacations
- Paid parking
- Sabbatical
- Paid membership in professional organizations

- Inclusion in a top club
- Small acts of recognition by a manager toward employees on a regular basis
- Continuous on-the-job training

Why Recognition Works

It's easy for a harried manager to overlook the consistent contributions of her staff. Recognition should be reserved for a major achievement; otherwise, it will lose its meaning. Right?

Wrong! A major achievement might be happening right under your nose. Yet you don't see it because there is no system in place to identify and reward solid, loyal performance. All too often, employees complain that their hard work, punctuality and years of service go unnoticed, while the awards go to higher-ranking managers and executives. Without recognition, their own performance becomes lackluster.

The first problem most companies need to address is how to train management to recognize employees' contributions. If you're a new manager in the department, review your staff's work history. Look for indications of company loyalty and hard work. Note employees who consistently arrive at work early or on time, who make helpful suggestions, and who see projects through to completion with little supervision. Look for people who take pride in their work and demonstrate a commitment to their jobs day in and day out, not just during a crisis.

Recognition is one of the easiest ways to increase productivity, because it boosts morale. To be effective, it should be accompanied by a symbol — an award that sets the employee apart from her peers. It can be as simple as a carnation or note of thanks to employees who pitched in on a project. It can be something more tangible that demonstrates the employee has been included in a club of top achievers. This can be:

- A certificate.

- A trophy.

- A plaque.

- A jacket (with team name or project name on it).

The only hard and fast rule of recognition is that it must reward real achievement. Ideally, it occurs when a specific goal has been reached or when an individual employee's effort serves as a motivating example to others. If you're wondering where to begin, take a lesson in recognition from a manufacturer on the East Coast that started its own "club" to recognize employee contributions.

"The 100 Club" worked on a system of annual accrual of points. Employees earned points in the following ways:

- Twenty-five points for a year of perfect attendance.

- Twenty points for a year without formal disciplinary action.

- Fifteen points for working a year without a lost-time injury.

- Five points deducted for each day or partial day of absence.

- Five to 20 points for cost-saving or safety suggestions.

- Five to 20 points for company-approved community service.

Employees who reached 100 points were rewarded with a jacket bearing the company logo and the words "The 100 Club." A simple act of recognition, but it worked. One of The 100 Club members modeled her jacket proudly at her local bank, announcing, "My employer gave me this for doing a good job. It's the first time in the 18 years I've been there that they've recognized the things I do every day."

To this employee, The 100 Club jacket was recognition for her work; the money she had earned wasn't.

Recognition works because it builds loyalty. You, as a manager, are rewarding loyalty with loyalty when you take the time to inquire about an employee's family. This simple act of recognition tells the employee you value her as an individual, not as a cog in the corporate machine, and that you understand people are your most valuable asset.

Here are some simple acts of recognition that really get the message across:

1. Know the names of all your employees. Never stumble when introducing them to visitors.

2. If they have children, know their names and ages.

3. Acknowledge watershed events: marriages, the birth of a child, a teenager's graduation from high school.

4. Write thank-you notes. The impact lasts longer than a verbal thank you. A proud employee can show it to friends and family.

5. Leave surprises on desks: carnations, cupcakes, chocolates, greeting cards.

6. When the pressure's on, pitch in. One boss serves her staff coffee and doughnuts when they've put in long, exhausting hours.

Simple acts of recognition are effective because employees see their genuineness. They don't feel manipulated by bosses, but appreciated by them. One employee described how recognition motivated her: "I have an expectation that if I do well, good things will happen to me."

What Kind of Recognition Works

Depending on your position in the company, you are able to institute various types of recognition. Only if you're a vice president or CEO, for example, will you have the means to provide the more lucrative symbols of recognition: the hefty paychecks and the generous expense accounts. Nevertheless, you should be aware of the different types of recognition and how they get results:

- Position in the company. This denotes title, power and rank. Professionals often have a strong identification with the company. Their position is tangible evidence of career achievement.

- Luxurious offices. Office size and location are frequently seen as symbols of an individual's authority and position in the company.

- Formal recognition of achievement. This can come from a CEO, a respected mentor, or from a leading expert in the individual's field. The more "professional" the source of recognition, the more valuable it is. The recognition can be given at a small ceremony, during a staff meeting, or at an annual awards banquet.

- Time off with pay. This can take the form of extra personal time, sabbaticals, or time off to attend professional meetings out of town.

- Paid membership in professional societies and paid subscriptions to professional journals. This translates as company support for staff specialists to get information from professional groups outside the company.

- Being taken to lunch. It's a small gesture, but it's an effective way of letting a staff member know you respect her as an individual, that she's special, that you're interested in her feedback, and you appreciate all her efforts on your behalf.

- Immediate rewards. When your staff has worked hard and helped you meet a tight deadline, act, don't talk. You can promise them annual bonuses, but, for the present, give them Friday afternoon off. You have repaid loyalty with loyalty. Taking action builds trust and credibility.

- Day-to-day recognition. Give loyal employees a day off or occasionally encourage them to take a long lunch. Stay in tune with their personal needs (enrolling in school, friends from out of town visiting, a relative's funeral) and reward them with a flexible work schedule.

- Expanded visibility. Some of your staff may be in the process of acquiring the skills or education that will increase their promotability. In the meantime, expand their visibility. Include them in meetings when it's appropriate. Make them feel important because they are.

- Training. You can do a lot to increase your staff's promotability by seeing that they are included in company training sessions. If your company doesn't offer training, initiate it.

- Shared information. You recognize your staff's importance when you share information about company changes with them. Seek their feedback. Act on their suggestions.

- Personalized tokens of appreciation. Take the time to find out the hobbies or interests of each person so you can customize your selection of tokens of appreciation. When employees receive something obviously selected for them personally based on their interests (as opposed to the standard certificate or whatever), the positive impact is multiplied exponentially.

Rewards for clerical workers and other support staff often take the form of recognition. As outlined above, it's a powerful motivator for staff because it reinforces the mutual respect between manager and employee.

When Recognition Doesn't Work

Ideally, recognition is a means of building trust and loyalty and ensuring better team effort by motivating employees. Recognition won't work, however, when it's not genuine; that is, when employees sense it's an alternative to giving them a well-deserved bonus or promotion. Depending on your company's reputation for fairness, recognition can be interpreted as a cheap way of buying off workers.

To keep recognition effective, make sure it fulfills the following objectives:

1. Don't substitute recognition for financial reward. If employees deserve a financial reward, make sure they get it.

2. Make sure a recognition party is effective. After enjoying a lavish dinner and awards presentation, it's not unusual for employees to complain, "The party was great considering how much it cost, but I would rather have had the money." Keep the objectives of the recognition party in view: to raise morale, lower tension, recognize individuals or teams who have made significant contributions. Don't spend money just to impress employees.

3. Reward promptly. When you've asked for extra effort, recognize and reward your staff promptly. Get in the habit of verbally recognizing employees on a regular basis for their commitment to their jobs.

Key Points

In this chapter, we've examined the most powerful motivator that managers can employ: recognition. It's also the least understood and most underutilized motivational tool.

- Recognition and financial bonuses are the two most commonly used rewards. To be most effective, they should be combined. The effect of financial rewards gradually wears off. Recognition, however, builds loyalty and trust.

- Recognition can be a simple gesture — a manager inquiring about an employee's family — or it can include symbols of achievement: a plaque, a certificate, a trophy, a team jacket.

- Be aware of the many different ways you can recognize employees and know when to commend them appropriately and effectively.

- Know when recognition isn't enough: when it's a substitute for deserved financial rewards, when it is not handled appropriately or fails to meet motivational objectives, or when the reward doesn't match what was asked for.

Set aside an hour or two to analyze the people who work for you. Examine what you know about each person. If you find that you don't know much, find out. You must have this information in order to create effective, individualized recognition items for each person on your team.

1. What is the most important thing in the world to this person? What is the least?

2. Names, ages, unique characteristics of family members.

3. Hobbies, particular points of interest.

4. Pet peeves.

5. What does this person enjoy the most?

6. What does she find funny? What type of sense of humor does this person have?

Based on the information you have generated, detail at least three personalized recognition items you can have ready when this person has earned one.

Reflections

7 PERFORMANCE: MOTIVATING WITH MONEY

Money can be a great motivator, as well as a great demotivator. It depends on how you handle it. Promotions, bonuses and raises all tell an employee that his contribution is appreciated and has value. But as we saw in the previous chapter, money works best when combined with recognition, the only motivator that gives an employee's work true meaning.

The power to reward is a basic way in which bosses influence subordinates. Bosses alone can confer raises, bonuses and pats on the back. Strangely enough, these incentives don't always motivate as they're intended to. They can breed hostility, distrust and unrest. By understanding how financial incentives work, you'll exercise your power to reward more effectively.

In this chapter, we'll look at the most common financial incentives, including raises, bonuses and other financial rewards, and when they get results and when they don't.

What Constitutes a Financial Incentive?

As discussed in the previous chapter, financial incentives are either rewards that encourage employees to reach certain predetermined goals, or job satisfiers used to attract talented candidates to your company. Typical financial incentives are raises and bonuses. Others are classified as employee benefits. Still others fall more under the category of perks, rather than actual money.

Financial incentives can be any of the following:

Rewards

- Cash incentives.

- Profit sharing.

- Employee benefits (paid vacations, sick leave).

- Scholarships.

- Rewards for helpful suggestions.

- Employee savings/retirement plans.

- Employee stock-ownership plans.

Perks

- Cruises.

- Paid membership in professional organizations.

- Paid parking.

- Sabbatical leaves.

Cash incentives can motivate employees to meet a difficult goal, especially when a company wants to dramatically increase sales or boost new products and services. Incentives, however, can encourage employees to compete against one another for short-term financial rewards. Company executives recommend using incentives judiciously and always accompanying them with verbal recognition so the employee's loyalty is reinforced.

Effective verbal recognition stresses the employee's achievement combined with thanks: "This is in recognition for the long hours and hard work you spent on that project. We couldn't have met our deadline without your help."

How to Make Raises Work

What could be better than a raise, particularly when an employee doesn't expect it? A raise should make both the manager and employee feel good about themselves. Unfortunately, it may fail to happen this way. When given the wrong way, the raise doesn't meet the employee's expectations. Its purpose backfires and the hard-working staffer thinks it's a sign the company doesn't recognize his efforts. This can happen when:

1. Management gives the standard raise the company recommends, without explaining that outstanding work on special projects is traditionally rewarded with bonuses.

2. Poor communication exists between management and staffers during the performance evaluation. Raises traditionally reflect the information exchanged about the employee's work performance during the annual performance review.

3. Management's language during the meeting is defensive: "I know it's not much, but ...", "I know it's not what you expected ... ."

4. The employee competes with peers for raises. When employees share information about raises, it usually results in feelings of being inadequately or unfairly compensated.

Avoid problems by keeping your objectives in sight. Raises usually are given during or immediately after the annual performance evaluation. This is your chance to concentrate on your team-building skills. Give recognition with the raise, share information and ask for employee feedback during the evaluation process. That way, you'll avoid hearing about employee dissatisfaction through the company grapevine. Remember to:

*   Put the raise in perspective. Most companies set a percentage increase each year for raises. When you're giving your employee his raise, share the big picture with him. Tell him his raise is consistent with the company-recommended standard. Then he'll be less disappointed if it is smaller than he hoped.

If there's a specific reason why the raise is smaller, explain it. "Company profits were down this year, so the standard raise was lowered from 10 percent to 7 percent. The board thinks this will help get the company back up to speed." Finally, if the employee has worked hard on a special project, recognize his effort and tell him when he can expect a bonus. Make good on your promise.

- Combine raises with feedback. Make sure the raise is consistent with the expectations established in the performance evaluation. The purpose of the raise is to make the employee feel good about his job. Even a raise of 4 or 5 percent, if handled the right way, can be viewed as an expression of appreciation.

Some bosses receive a chunk of money to be divided among their employees as raises. They decide how the money is distributed, tying merit raises to meeting performance goals. For top achievers, give plenty of recognition. "You've done such a terrific job this year, we're giving you more than the standard raise." Nothing motivates a top performer to keep going like recognition and reward.

For underachievers: Let them know why they're getting less. Be positive and constructive. This can give them the motivation to turn their work around. Make sure there are no surprises. This information should follow a detailed performance review and running dialogue about the employee's work. Set clear objectives about what the employee must do to earn a better raise in the future.

- Watch your language. It's difficult not to become defensive, particularly if an employee is angry or upset about his raise. Keep cool. Explain the circumstances, but don't apologize for them. Be empathetic; use active listening when the discussion becomes a debate. State your understanding of the employee's emotions, then restate your position: "I understand your disappointment over an 8 percent raise when you were expecting 10 percent. As I said, the company is restructuring right now. Hopefully, we can repay your loyalty and hard work more generously next year."

- Match raises to performance. You can discourage, but not prevent, employees from sharing information about raises. When employees become envious or dissatisfied, explain that their raise was tied to their job performance. Motivate them to improve their performance in the coming year by recognizing what they do well. Give them objectives to work toward.

How to Make Bonuses Work

Traditionally, bonuses have been used to reward high-level executives, sales staff and other employees whose contributions directly affect the company's bottom line.

Yet, today's managers recognize bonuses as an effective way to reward team effort and to motivate less visible staff members. Here are some essential do's and don'ts regarding bonuses:

1. Never make bonuses automatic. Bonuses lose their value if they're given out so routinely that employees come to expect them. They are rewards only for outstanding effort.

2. Make bonuses timely. Give bonuses when they are deserved and as close to the results you are rewarding as possible. A bonus given six months after completion of a project loses its motivational power.

3. Reward team effort with bonuses. When the goals have been met by team effort, reward the team as a whole. Give equal bonuses to each team member.

4. Lighten an oppressive workload with bonuses. The head of an East Coast publishing company hands out cash on the spot to boost his employees' morale during busy periods. "When we're working on a monstrous project or we have a crazy schedule, bonuses lighten the tension in the air."

When Incentives Don't Work

Some companies are totally opposed to cash incentives. They claim that quality is sacrificed to quantity, and that employees end up competing against one another rather than working as a team. Cash incentives, however, aren't intrinsically good or bad. They're motivational tools. Enlightened managerial philosophy, or lack of it, determines their effectiveness.

Take it from a CEO who started his own overnight delivery service. During its first six years, the company grew 8,100 percent. It had $17 million in sales, while the rest of the trucking industry had shrunk by two-thirds. How did this monumental growth occur? By a highly structured system of incentives.

Yet, the president found himself surrounded by distrustful managers, dissatisfied dockworkers and an unhappy sales staff. His thirst for growth had pushed employees to get their bonuses any way they could, even if it meant falsifying delivery and dock-loading receipts. As one vice president noted, "There was no common thread. Everyone was motivated by their own incentives."

The CEO responded by abolishing the intricate sales-incentive structure. He decided to start from scratch and organize his top people as a team. They began by writing a statement of corporate purpose. "The process forced us to think through our priorities," stated the CEO. The new mission statement concentrated on providing employees with an environment that "promotes joy at work and achievement of personal goals."

When incentives don't work, it's usually because employees feel that their employer is using them. Bosses appear to be "master manipulators" who view employees as a means to achieve certain ends. Used this way, incentives destroy team unity and company loyalty because they act as bribes for good performance, rather than as motivators.

Employees react by:

1. Rebelling and cheating the system.

2. Leaving the company.

3. Refusing to make the extra effort.

Incentives work as long as they don't take the place of traditional motivators: team building, recognition and broader rewards. If your company requires immense dedication from employees, use cash incentives sparingly over the short term and always combine them with recognition.

Alternative Financial Rewards

Innovative companies are finding ways to make money work for them. Not by spending it on employees, but by investing it in their employees.

Take Johnsonville Foods, a specialty-foods and sausage-making company in Sheboygan, Wisconsin. Instead of a personnel department, Johnsonville has a Personal Development Lifelong Learning Department. Here employees meet with counselors who help them articulate goals and dreams. They can be as varied as learning to grow roses or putting a child through college.

Each employee then receives a $100 annual allowance to spend on a personal growth project. Some join cooking classes. Others use the money to help meet big expenses like education.

It's hardly surprising that Johnsonville experiences little turnover and its sales have risen a steady 15 percent annually. "We view people as an appreciating asset," said one vice president. The rewards system Johnsonville uses doesn't run the risk of alienating employees because:

1. The rewards stress personal growth and development rather than competition.

2. The rewards motivate because they're part of a bigger management philosophy that values and recognizes employees.

3. The rewards are uniform. Everyone gets the same amount. The employees can use the money any way they like.

4. The rewards are not manipulative. Employees don't feel pressure by the company to work harder to meet company goals that negate their personal goals.

5. Company goals and employee goals are in sync. Therefore, rewards act as fulfillments, not bribes.

American business has a lot to learn from companies like Johnsonville Foods. Money talks but, to act as a true reward, it also has to nurture employees.

Key Points

In this chapter, we've discussed when financial rewards work and when they don't.

1. Raises work:

   - When the standard company raise is explained to the employee.

   - When information about the company's financial picture is shared.

   - When they are fair and consistent with the performance evaluation.

2. Bonuses work:

   - When they're not automatic.

   - When they're timely.

   - When they stress personal growth and development.

   - When they reward a specific project.

   - As motivators to help employees get through a work crunch.

3. Incentives work:

    - When they're short-term.

    - When they're not manipulative.

    - When quantity doesn't threaten quality.

1. Identify how you can make the raises you give your employees more effective motivators. Outline the steps you will take in presenting the next round of raises to them.

2. If you have a bonus system in place, evaluate its effectiveness as a motivational tool for improving performance. What needs to be improved? Who has the authority to make the necessary changes?

   If you have no bonus program, what would it take to put one in place? How could you justify it? What types of performance improvements would make such a plan worthwhile?

3. Review the Johnsonville Foods incentive program. What could you put in place for your people to build their trust and loyalty and to enhance their performance? What would it take to put a program into place? What are you waiting for?

Reflections

8 POTENTIAL MOTIVATIONAL PROBLEMS: THE NEWLY HIRED

The road to hiring the right people is never smooth and straight. You have to find qualified candidates. That may mean combing the leading business schools and colleges. Depending on your recruiting budget, you might spend days or even weeks wining and dining them, taking them to baseball games, showing them the best the city and your company have to offer. Then, after lengthy negotiations, you make an offer. And they accept.

But your managerial job has only begun. Too often, a new recruit, full of enthusiasm and effervescence, shows up for work ready to take on the world. Instead, she's shown her desk and told to tackle a mindless task that would bore a third-grader. After a month or so, your new recruit is looking distracted and vaguely dissatisfied. After six months, she's gone and the whole process starts again.

In this chapter, we'll look at the critical stages of a new hire's introduction to the workplace and how you and your company can make it better. We'll examine:

- The job interview.

- The first day.

- On-the-job training.

- Frequent performance appraisals.

Finding and Hiring Exceptional People

Finding and hiring a good employee is expensive; losing one costs you double.

Consider the expenses involved in filling a staff support position:

1. Advertising.

2. Staff time spent interviewing.

3. Staff time spent checking references and evaluating.

4. Staff time spent filling out benefit forms.

5. Orientation and training.

And as you know, the cost of filling higher-level positions is much greater, sometimes as much as $80,000 to hire and train a professional employee.

A quick look at the bottom line will tell you that it's in your company's favor to keep newly hired people motivated. Yet, few companies realize that the first few days on the job, even the first few hours, mold the new recruit's attitude about her employer for years to come.

Before beginning your recruiting efforts, be sure you have completed a full job audit.

- Specifically, what are the duties required to complete the job?

- What tools, services and/or accommodations are needed to complete these duties?

- Who supervises the employee in this position?

- With which other people does this person interact, both in and out of the organization?

- Can all duties be completed in the time allotted?

- What formal training does a person need to perform this job satisfactorily?

- What technical, interpersonal, organizational and problem-solving skills does the person need to complete this job?

- What is the evaluation criteria and process?

Now that the job audit is completed, you are ready to begin your interviewing process.

The Job Interview

It's natural for potential employees to be anxious to make a good impression during a job interview. But it's also your chance, as their prospective manager, to make a lasting impression on them. Research shows that employees often leave a company in a year or two unless they've been thoroughly prepared for what the job and the company require. Here are some ways you can turn the job interview into a challenge that motivates qualified candidates:

1. Be upbeat and professional in your demeanor and appearance. Make a good impression and it will reflect well on your company. Don't resort to cynicism or making jokes about the company. New job candidates want to work for someone they like and respect and who is enthusiastic about her job and employer.

2. Describe the company's history and philosophy. This is your chance to sell your job candidate on the company you work for. Tell her why you're proud to be part of this outfit. Share the company vision. Fill her in on:

    - Outstanding company achievements. "We were the first computer company to work with NASA in putting a man on the moon."

- The financial health of the company. Provide a copy of the annual report, etc.

- Where the company is headed, including what new markets you'll be exploring in the next decade, or how the company business is diversifying or consolidating.

- How the company reflects the innovative leadership of its owners and what part they've had in shaping company philosophy. If there's something about the company that excites you and makes you proud, tell her. "We want to avoid employee burnout. We introduced flextime; now we have job sharing. We're instituting sabbatical leaves for employees who've been with us for a minimum of five years."

3. Be honest about the job requirements. Make sure the prospective employee is given correct information regarding the duties and benefits of the position. Let her know what to expect. Be specific. If it means three nights of travel a week, say so. Don't make impossible promises you can't fulfill.

4. Communicate clearly what you're looking for in a candidate. Maybe you need people who are innovative and creative, or perhaps you value organization and loyalty. Tell your candidate about your personal values, what you think makes a good employee. That way, there will be no surprises the first day on the job.

   Be sure to evaluate the candidate in numerous areas including educational background, related work experience, specific skills and overall attitudes, career objectives, work views and philosophies.

5. Get her feedback. Don't get so carried away with your speech that you don't allow her to interrupt, ask questions or comment freely. You may have missed or glossed over some important points. The more give-and-take between the two of you, the better you'll know your prospective employee when the interview is over. Ask her what she's looking for in a job and in a company.

This is your chance to impress the job candidate with your company's professionalism, friendliness and efficiency.

The First Day

The first day on a job is like the first day at an unfamiliar school. You're the new kid on the block. Everyone else appears to know their jobs and each other. It's an uncomfortable feeling for new recruits.

The first day on the job is of crucial importance, not only in making new employees feel at home, but in helping them make necessary connections with key employees and telling them their specific duties. One businesswoman estimated that she had worked in nearly 20 firms, corporations and institutions; none had ever spent more than a few hours in preparing her for her position in the organization.

To avoid causing your new employee to think twice about the position she has accepted, make sure the following bases are covered:

1. The personnel department. Minimize the amount of time a new employee has to spend parked in the personnel department. If it's imperative for her to sign forms, have her do it in your office or at her desk. Make sure the paperwork is handled deftly and graciously. Too often, new recruits lose their motivation when they are left in personnel for much of the first day.

2. Her desk/office. Be sure your new recruit knows where to hang her hat and how to unlock her desk. Show her the phone and the employee phone list. But, once again, don't just leave her there. Keep her motivated by keeping her in motion.

3. Assign a guide. Assign someone to guide your new employee through the first day. This person can introduce her to her peers and key people she'll need to know: vice presidents, department heads, other managers. Show her where the amenities are: bathrooms, break room, cafeteria, elevators. Introduce the new

employee to the receptionist to ensure she will be recognized as an official staff member. Make a personal effort to see that she gets settled in.

4. Lunch. Take your new staffer to lunch. Let her relax while you do the talking. Share with her the general game plan for the next few weeks. Tell her about orientation and/or training programs she'll be attending. Give her a sense of direction and purpose. Give her support and encouragement.

Ideally, after the first day your new employee, motivated by a sense of inclusion, will approach job responsibilities with enthusiasm. It is crucial, however, that from day one new hires feel they're part of the team effort to reach the firm's goals.

On-the-Job Training

Training can consist of anything from slowly building knowledge and expertise to highly structured training lasting anywhere from six months to a year. The purpose of training is not only to acquaint the employee with her job responsibilities, but also to teach:

1. Company policies and procedures.

2. Company expectations (dress code, ethics code, etc.) and culture.

3. Safety procedures.

Managers need to be aware that it takes time for an employee to learn a job. Allow extra time in training to master a learning curve that can involve mistakes and adjustments. A manager's responsibility to a new employee is twofold:

1. To teach the specifics of the new job.

2. To acquaint the new employee with the corporate culture.

Companies disagree about what constitutes effective training and/or orientation. The purpose is to keep the new recruits' motivation high while building their knowledge and job skills. Two methods of training that make employees comfortable and productive at a new job are:

1. Mentoring.

2. Cross-training.

Mentoring

In some companies, new recruits are paired with a senior executive who acts as a trainer. Mentors not only ensure that employees get day-to-day guidance and information, but also exert a socializing influence — making sure the new recruit meets like-minded employees. One ad agency in Chicago assigns two mentors to every new professional:

1. The senior mentor. This trainer is usually at least seven years along in her career. She gives the new recruit advice and shows her how the job is done.

2. The junior mentor. This mentor is closer to the employee's age and status and has usually had just one or two years of training herself. She's assigned to provide encouragement, support and identity. She also acts as a social connection.

When assigning mentors, managers should be careful to select employees who possess not only solid on-the-job experience, but also cheerful, outgoing dispositions. The mentors should be true believers in the system and willing and ready to volunteer their time and advice. The wrong mentor can act as a big demotivator to a new recruit, especially if that mentor falls prey to any of the three deadly sins of mentoring.

Three Deadly Sins of Mentoring

- Neglect. A mentor must commit the time necessary. A minimum of one meeting per month with more frequent phone or e-mail contact is to be anticipated.

- Breach of confidentiality. "Leaks" will quickly kill a mentoring relationship and demotivate the new employee.

- Insensitivity to differences. Both parties must pick up on cultural, race and gender differences. A little background work and good listening skills go a long way.

Cross-Training

At a well-run manufacturing company in Cleveland, newly hired MBAs roll up their sleeves and go to welding school for 10 months. The idea is to cross-train the people who will be in powerful positions in every area of the welding business. Company owners figure the payoff is company executives who make responsible decisions based on a wide range of experiences. The training continues for a year, with employees receiving instruction in communication and other managerial arts from practitioners within the company. Steeping their MBAs in manufacturing, as well as the corporate culture, has paid off for the Cleveland company. The people making the decisions in the executive boardroom are more informed, more sympathetic to the manufacturing side of the business, and tend to see issues in the round, rather than from a purely financial angle.

Frequent Performance Appraisals

Being interactive is a good way to keep new recruits motivated. According to one business insider, "If you don't pay attention to them, you lose them very easily."

Make sure the new employee is getting the feedback she needs through frequent performance appraisals: quarterly is not too often during the first one or two years on the job. Ease performance fears by explaining it's your way of making sure she stays happy and excels at her job. Here are some guidelines to follow:

1. Applaud what she's doing right frequently and publicly. Give plenty of positive feedback; she's learning a whole new culture. "You've caught on quickly to these marketing research techniques. I'm very pleased with your progress."

2. Coach her on what she's doing wrong. Give emotional support while correcting her. "We handle this procedure a little differently. I realize it's complicated, so Sally here will take you through it a couple more times. Please go to her with any questions you have."

3. Ask for feedback. Show that you are eager to learn from her, as well as teach her. "I've got some time on Wednesday and I'd like you to tell me about how you structured that statistical survey. It sounds intriguing. I'm sure you've got questions, so be sure to ask me anything you don't understand."

4. Establish how you can best help her with her learning curve.

Key Points

Remember that once you've gone to all the trouble to get a new employee, it's in your best interest to keep her. Here are the key ways in which you can be most effective in motivating the newly hired:

1. Complete a job audit before you begin the interviewing process.

2. During the job interview:

   • Be upbeat and professional.

   • Fill her in on the company history.

   • Be honest about the job requirements.

   • Tell her what you're looking for in an employee.

- Ask her what she's looking for.

- Assess the candidate's background, experience and attitudes.

3. During the first day:

- Involve her in office life immediately.

- Show her her desk, her office.

- Assign a guide.

- Introduce her to your department, your staff.

- Take her to lunch.

4. On-the-job training:

- Provide her with mentors.

- If available, provide her with cross-training.

5. During the first year, offer frequent performance appraisals:

- Applaud what she's doing right.

- Coach her on what she's doing wrong.

- Ask her for — and listen to — her feedback.

1. Complete a job audit on every position reporting to you. A job description is not sufficient. Go back and review each question on pages 82 and 83 and do a detailed assessment to assist you in placing and keeping the best qualified individuals in each position.

2. Review your interviewing techniques. Are you completely comfortable with the process, and does your track record indicate you make good selections? In what areas could you make improvements? Make a list of these areas, then prioritize them. What one change in your interviewing would make the biggest difference?

3. Outline what an ideal "first day on the job" would be for you. What kinds of support and activities would help you adjust most effectively? What questions would you want answered? Identify both the questions you would ask and those you would be uncomfortable asking.

   Compare your ideal to the process your recruits experience on their first day. What changes/improvements could you make to the process to make them more at ease and more productive quickly?

4. Assess your current on-the-job training. How could you include (or improve) a mentoring element and cross-training? How frequently are formal performance appraisals conducted in the first year? Informal ones? Is this the optimum schedule for achieving peak performance? Adjust your schedule accordingly.

Reflections

9 PERFORMANCE PROBLEMS: EMPLOYEE BURNOUT

It's considered normal for employees, who are enthusiastic and highly motivated when they start new jobs, to lose some of their momentum as the years go by. According to a recent survey, 53 percent of first-year employees said they were highly committed to their jobs. That percentage dropped to 34 percent for employees who had been in the same job for four years or more.

Although a certain amount of employee burnout may be normal, a serious slowdown in commitment and dedication could ultimately cost a company its competitive edge. As a manager, you're responsible for creating a climate that's conducive to motivation, which is not a problem when there's a new project to tackle or when your people are eager and willing to show their stuff. The issue becomes more complicated when you are dealing with employees who outrank you in seniority or have been numbed by routine, or when you're trying to stabilize turnover among minimum-wage workers.

Dealing with employee burnout requires special managerial skills. In this chapter we'll explore:

- How to recognize employee burnout.

- How to motivate long-term employees.

- How to motivate low-wage employees.

How to Recognize Employee Burnout

Maybe you've rationalized your department's low productivity as a temporary slump, and maybe you're right. However, you may find that your sagging profitability has something to do with employees feeling derailed and unmotivated.

Here are some warning signs of impending employee burnout:

- Feeling that they make no difference.

- Petty personal disagreements.

- Lack of enthusiasm.

- Inconsistency.

- Emotional mood swings.

- Depression/anxiety.

- Chronic fatigue/mental fatigue.

- Chronic infections (colds, flu, etc.).

What causes employee burnout? Eight specific types of situations lead to the majority of the burnout situations:

- A critical boss.

- A perpetually dissatisfied client or customer.

- Lack of recognition.

- Ambiguity.

- Unending tasks.

- No-win situations.

- Overload.

- Feeling trapped.

Possibly the biggest cause of demotivation in an employee is a feeling of being trapped, that his career is going nowhere. Lack of autonomy or control over one's working conditions is a big demotivator and more common among low-wage workers than higher-ranking executives.

It could be that certain members of your team are badly in need of a heart-to-heart talk with the coach to revitalize their energies.

Here's what you can do:

1. Be a good listener. When there's a specific problem (low sales figures, little productivity), invite employees to talk about it. Try not to criticize. Listen empathetically. You might get some vital information that will help you solve a problem and better understand an employee.

2. Be a good coach. Give the employee feedback. Let him know that the company cares about him, and that he's critical to the team effort to meet goals. Compliment him on something he does well.

3. Make work fun. Researchers are finding that having fun at work increases productivity. The key is to make work feel like play. Encourage the employee to approach problems as games, and he'll come up with better solutions than people who approach problems as work. Workers who report having fun at work:

   - Are absent or late to work less often.

   - Meet work demands more effectively.

   - Are more creative at problem solving.

   - Are less depressed and more satisfied with their lives in general.

How to Motivate Long-Term Employees

Any manager will tell you that the more years people spend in the same job, the more you need to reinforce to them that they're important to the company.

It's not unusual for long-term employees to outrank their managers in number of years with the company. Yet, despite their experience, they may suffer from low self-esteem if they have little control over their working lives. A savvy manager can counteract lack of motivation by judicious distribution of recognition and rewards. Take a look at your long-term staffer and ask yourself:

1. How many years has he been in his present job?

2. How large a salary increase has he received over those years?

3. How many people does he have reporting to him?

4. Have his work responsibilities increased?

5. Has he been given significant workload expansion?

6. How much departmental contact does he have with peers? With higher-ups?

7. Does he receive recognition and rewards for his work? With what frequency?

Let your long-term employee know how much you and the company appreciate him. Maybe you don't have the money in your budget to give him a badly needed bonus or payroll boost, but here are some acts of managerial recognition that get the message across:

1. Broaden his planning responsibility. Let your staffer set his own standards and objectives. If he has subordinates, delegate more control to him.

2. Get him involved in departmental problem solving. Team meetings are a good way to start. If he has an area of expertise, use that as the basis for his inclusion. Ask for his contributions in brainstorming sessions.

3. Broaden his learning base. If he's a clerk, train him to do part of the buyer's duties; if he's a line worker, give him some management tasks. Cross-train him in other areas within the company that complement his basic expertise.

4. When he contributes ideas and opinions, reward him with recognition. Get his name in the company newsletter; put his suggestion, along with others, in a memo on the company bulletin board.

5. Increase his contact with peers and other bosses in the company. Allow him the freedom to laterally network with other departments.

6. Allow him time and space to develop innovative thinking. If it looks like your long-term employee is achieving outstanding productivity, don't load him down with trivial paperwork. Give him some room to develop action plans and goal-setting procedures. Support him in company meetings when he makes contributions.

Recently, IBM had to decide what to do with long-term employees it no longer had jobs for in manufacturing, development and administration. Rather than terminate them or give them an extended leave without pay, IBM solved its problem in an innovative manner that benefited both the company and its employees: it put them where they were needed. IBM called this move "redeployment." Despite their incompatible backgrounds, the company shifted 21,500 employees into marketing and programming and another 11,800 into sales.

The results? Cross-training paid off. According to one IBM executive, "The redeployed people were just as successful in the field as new hires, if not more so."

Despite dire predictions, long-term "techies" took to sales like ducks to water. IBM recently instituted the 100 Percent Club for salespeople who achieved their quotas and proudly announced that 70 percent of those in sales were club members. The lesson IBM has to teach managers is to stretch jobs for long-term employees to offer variety and growth. Any job becomes stale after a few years. When the thrill wears off, motivation lags. Managers can avoid this by:

1. Creating opportunities for the long-term employee to learn new skills.

2. Shifting assignments and responsibilities.

How to Motivate Low-Wage Employees

Your low-wage employees are your company's foot soldiers. Just as an army couldn't win a battle without its infantry, your minimum-wage workers are in the trenches, dealing with customer complaints, soothing irate buyers, and smiling courteously when a disgruntled customer demands their names and says, "I want to talk to your supervisor."

How does a manager compensate his low-wage workers' loyalty? How does he recognize them effectively when keeping them motivated is difficult?

Low-wage jobs are generally perceived as dead-end jobs. They require long hours of monotonous work with few or no inherent job satisfiers. Not only is the money lacking, but so are traditional perks and lush benefits. Few people admire or respect low-wage workers. All of these factors add up to make your job as a motivating manager of low-wage workers even more challenging.

Showing your employees that you like and respect them does a lot to overcome built-in demotivators. You can make your employees feel that they're special by instilling an esprit de corps that gives them an identity and makes them proud to be on a team. Do this by:

1. Making work a fun place to be. Keep productivity and spirits high by encouraging self-expression and creativity. Encourage employees to put out their own newsletter, adopt a community charity, play on a company softball team, etc.

2. Establishing recognition awards for the most motivated employee of the month. Post the employee's picture where customers can see it. If he's won the award for two or more months in a row, make the award special.

3. Cross-training employees. Help workers overcome monotony by training them at other jobs and rotating them regularly, even within a single shift.

4. Organizing team-building events after work. Send your employees to motivational seminars, or plan an annual awards banquet or picnic. Make the event one that both rewards and challenges them.

5. Setting up a scholarship fund. Through raffles, donations or matching funds from the company, reward scholarships to outstanding employees who are attending college part time. Communicate to your employees that the job is a means for them to meet personal goals.

6. Listening and giving positive feedback. Be there when they need someone to talk to; otherwise, they'll voice their discontent elsewhere.

Ask yourself, "What can I do to make these people like themselves better in their jobs?" The answer lies in teaching them to respect their jobs by working for a manager who respects them. During team meetings, include your workers in bottom-line statistics. Show them how much they've contributed to overall productivity. Ask them to develop their own action plans for increasing revenues.

Don't forget to use humor when it's positively directed: incorporate jokes, laughter, even employee-generated cartoons. Humor shared within a group tends to:

1. Defuse tension.

2. Make meetings more productive.

3. Heighten individual creativity.

You know about the part of your employees' jobs you can't change, the part that burns them out. Concentrate on what you can do to make their jobs better, more fun and more rewarding. Workers who enjoy their jobs suffer less boredom and conflict and, therefore, perform better than workers who hate their jobs.

Key Points

- Employee burnout has clear warning signs and wake-up calls. An astute manager will be on the lookout for these signals.

- Various types of situations are prone to promoting burnout: overly critical management and customers; no-win situations; ambiguity; lack of control; unending, monotonous tasks; lack of recognition; being overloaded and overwhelmed.

- Ways to motivate the long-term employee would include:

    1. Broadening the employee's planning responsibility.

    2. Involving the employee in departmental problem solving.

    3. Broadening his learning base through training.

    4. Rewarding his contributions with recognition.

    5. Increasing his contact with peers and superiors.

    6. Giving him the space and time to develop innovative ideas.

- The biggest motivator for low-wage employees is your respect for them as individuals. You can communicate this by being creative about the way you reward your workers and by making their working environment as stimulating and stress-free as possible.

1. Are your employees going about their tasks with a noticeable lack of enthusiasm?

2. Are your employees easily distracted from their work?
   - Spending time on personal phone calls.
   - Taking long lunches.
   - Making interoffice social visits.
   - Missing deadlines.
   - Not setting goals.

3. In conversation, are they dwelling on off-the-job problems?
   - Family matters.
   - Conflicting priorities.
   - Health problems.

4. When you correct them, are they hostile and quick to anger?
   - Do they take criticism personally?
   - Are they rebellious and political?

5. Are some employees becoming more private and withdrawn?
   - Less alert.
   - Absent-minded.
   - Tense and irritable when they're encouraged to communicate.

Now that you've identified the problem areas, what are you going to do about them?

Reflections

10 MOTIVATING YOUR EMPLOYEES TO PEAK PERFORMANCE — A REVIEW

A manager's job of motivating employees is never finished. That's because motivation takes place on a day-by-day basis. Employees watch their bosses carefully. Ideally, they'd like their managers to be role models, educators, understanding friends and visionary leaders. The best way to motivate your employees is by communicating your respect for them as individuals and providing a caring environment in which they can work. Here are the six best ways to motivate your employees.

1. Leadership. You can't motivate by words that lack conviction or isolated actions that lack follow-through. Each day you walk into the office, you demonstrate anew your purpose, your convictions and your commitment to be the best. Employees can tell when you're handing them a line and when you live, breathe and believe what you say. Make your behavior consistent with what you tell employees. Learn to discern the difference between external motivators (financial incentives and rewards for working toward a short-term goal) and internal motivators (words and recognition that build self-esteem). When you're internally motivated, your employees trust you to be consistent, fair-minded and true to your system of values.

2. Team building. Good coaches build strong teams. Playing on a team teaches employees how to sublimate individual rewards for the good of the group. It also gives them the experience of learning to play by the rules and perform well in the position that capitalizes

on their strengths. They learn to win with modesty and lose with grace. A good coach sets goals, communicates strategy clearly, and creates a strong team identity. Managers motivate employees by recognizing their individual talents and making them a vital part of the overall team effort.

3. Delegation. To delegate well, managers must know not only when to delegate, but what to delegate. Some managers wait until they've reached the breaking point to hand over work to an employee. Do it before your workload buries you and before your talented employees become bored.

   Nothing motivates good employees like delegation. They feel respected, included and trusted to perform well. Delegate in a timely, efficient manner that allows you time to communicate what you need to your employee and to monitor the results.

   Never dump unwanted work and call it delegation. Delegate tasks that will stretch your employee's abilities and hone her promotable skills. Always delegate the authority needed to complete the delegated task. Give your employee your full backing and support.

4. Communication. In order for your communication to motivate your employees, you must be credible. This means having a good track record, presenting a visual image that's congruent with your spoken message, and being enthusiastic. One way to motivate employees effectively is to be generous with information. Never hoard it. Give them plenty of feedback on company decisions, changes in directions and how overall priorities have changed. When correcting employees, be sure you give emotional support simultaneously. Communicate in a manner that stresses appreciation for your employees' positive contributions. Avoid too much criticism; it's a big demotivator.

5. Recognition. Recognition is the most potent kind of reward because it stimulates an internal motivator, your employee's self-esteem. Recognition can take many forms, such as: a picture of your

employee shaking hands with the CEO, remembering to inquire about an employee's family, or rewarding a hard-working employee with a simple gift and thank-you note for a job well done. Recognition communicates appreciation from an employee's company and manager. It builds loyalty because it honors employees as a company's most valuable asset.

6. Financial incentives. When used sparingly, financial incentives, such as bonuses, can help a company reach short-term goals by boosting productivity. Financial incentives are no replacement for internal motivators, and employees should not become dependent on bonuses to work their hardest. When cash incentives are the favorite method of reward, quality is often sacrificed for quantity; team spirit gives way to individual competitiveness. Make raises work for you as a motivator, not against you. Always accompany financial incentives with personal recognition, whether words of appreciation or awards banquets.

Showing your employees that you respect them, that their company cares about them, is the biggest motivator of all. One way companies do this is by becoming family-friendly, responding to employees' needs for greater flexibility in arranging their workday to help manage their families.

Surprisingly, the amount of pleasure your workers derive from their jobs doesn't depend so much on the job, its pay structure or the length of time they've done it. It depends on how much you, their manager, can communicate a sense of respect and commitment by making their jobs fun, invigorating and varied, and, therefore, motivating experiences.

Go for it! It's well worth the effort.

RECOMMENDED READING

Bruce, Ann, and James S. Pepitone. *Motivating Employees*, 1998.

Canfield, Jack. *Heart at Work: Stories and Strategies for Building Self-Esteem and Reawakening the Soul at Work*, 1998.

Crane, Thomas G. *The Heart of Coaching: Using Transformational Coaching to Create a High-Performance Culture*, 1998.

Hiam, Alexander. *Motivating and Rewarding Employees: New and Better Ways to Improve Your People*, 1999.

Hughes, Marylou. *Keeping Your Job While Your Bosses Are Losing Theirs*, 1998.

Kinlaw, Dennis C. *Coaching for Commitment: Interpersonal Strategies for Obtaining Superior Performance from Individuals and Teams*, 1999.

Rey, David. *1001 Ways to Inspire: Your Organization, Your Team and Yourself*, 1998.

Sims, Ronald E. *Keys to Employee Success in Coming Decades*, 1999.

INDEX

Notes

Notes

Notes

Notes

Notes

Notes

Buy any 3, get 1 FREE!

Get a 60-Minute Training Series™ Handbook FREE ($14.95 value)* when you buy any three. See back of order form for full selection of titles.

These are helpful how-to books for you, your employees and co-workers. Add to your library. Use for new-employee training, brown-bag seminars, promotion gifts and more. Choose from many popular titles on a variety of lifestyle, communication, productivity and leadership topics exclusively from National Press Publications.

BUY 3 GET 1 FREE!
Buy more, save more!

DESKTOP HANDBOOK ORDER FORM

Ordering is easy:

1. Complete both sides of this Order Form, detach, and mail, fax or phone your order to:

Mail:	National Press Publications
	P.O. Box 419107
	Kansas City, MO 64141-6107
Fax:	1-913-432-0824
Phone:	1-800-258-7248
Internet:	www.NationalSeminarsTraining.com

2. Please print:

Name_____ Position/Title _____

Company/Organization_____

Address_____City _____

State/Province_____ZIP/Postal Code _____

Telephone (____)_____ Fax (____) _____

Your e-mail: _____

3. Easy payment:

❑ Enclosed is my check or money order for $_____ (total from back).
   Please make payable to National Press Publications.

Please charge to:

❑ MasterCard   ❑ VISA   ❑ American Express

Credit Card No. _____ Exp. Date_____

Signature_____

• •

MORE WAYS TO SAVE:

SAVE 33%!!! BUY 20-50 COPIES of any title ... pay just $9.95 each ($13.25 Canadian).

SAVE 40%!!! BUY 51 COPIES OR MORE of any title ... pay just $8.95 each ($11.95 Canadian).

* $20.00 in Canada

Buy 3, get 1 FREE!

60-MINUTE TRAINING SERIES™ HANDBOOKS

TITLE	ITEM #	RETAIL PRICE*	QTY	TOTAL
8 Steps for Highly Effective Negotiations	#424	$14.95		
Assertiveness	#4422	$14.95		
Balancing Career and Family	#4152	$14.95		
Common Ground	#4122	$14.95		
Delegate for Results	#4592	$14.95		
The Essentials of Business Writing	#4310	$14.95		
Everyday Parenting Solutions	#4862	$14.95		
Exceptional Customer Service	#4882	$14.95		
Fear & Anger: Slay the Dragons …	#4302	$14.95		
Fundamentals of Planning	#4301	$14.95		
Getting Things Done	#4112	$14.95		
How to Coach an Effective Team	#4308	$14.95		
How to De-Junk Your Life	#4306	$14.95		
How to Handle Conflict and Confrontation	#4952	$14.95		
How to Manage Your Boss	#493	$14.95		
How to Supervise People	#4102	$14.95		
How to Work With People	#4032	$14.95		
Inspire & Motivate: Performance Reviews	#4232	$14.95		
Listen Up: Hear What's Really Being Said	#4172	$14.95		
Motivation and Goal-Setting	#4962	$14.95		
A New Attitude	#4432	$14.95		
The New Dynamic Comm. Skills for Women	#4309	$14.95		
The Polished Professional	#4262	$14.95		
The Power of Innovative Thinking	#428	$14.95		
The Power of Self-Managed Teams	#4222	$14.95		
Powerful Communication Skills	#4132	$14.95		
Present With Confidence	#4612	$14.95		
The Secret to Developing Peak Performers	#4692	$14.95		
Self-Esteem: The Power to Be Your Best	#4642	$14.95		
Shortcuts to Organized Files & Records	#4307	$14.95		
The Stress Management Handbook	#4842	$14.95		
Supreme Teams: How to Make Teams Work	#4303	$14.95		
Thriving on Change	#4212	$14.95		
Women and Leadership	#4632	$14.95		

Sales Tax
All purchases subject to
state and local sales tax.
Questions?
Call
1-800-258-7248

Subtotal	$
Add 7% Sales Tax (*Or add appropriate state and local tax*)	$
Shipping and Handling** (*$6 one item; 50¢ each additional item*)	$
TOTAL	$

**Free Freight on all orders over $150.00   * $20.00 in Canada